For Every Tatter

For Every Tatter

Christine H. Boldt

LITERARY PRESS
LAMAR UNIVERSITY

ISBN: 978-1-942956-84-6
Library of Congress Control Number: 2021932001
Manufactured in the United States

Lamar University Literary Press
Beaumont, Texas

For Paul

Recent Poetry from Lamar University Literary Press

Lisa Adams, *Xuai*
Bobby Aldridge, *An Affair of the Stilled Heart*
Michael Baldwin, *Lone Star Heart, Poems of a Life in Texas*
Charles Behlen, *Failing Heaven*
David Bowles, *Flower, Song, Dance: Aztec and Mayan Poetry*
Jerry Bradley, *Collapsing into Possibility*
Jerry Bradley, *Crownfeathers and Effigies*
Jerry Bradley and Ulf Kirchdorfer, editors, *The Great American Wise Ass Poetry Anthology*
Matthew Brennan, *One Life*
Mark Busby, *Through Our Times*
Julie Chappell, *Mad Habits of a Life*
Stan Crawford, *Resisting Gravity*
Chip Dameron, *Waiting for an Etcher*
Glover Davis, *My Mad Cap of Darkness*
William Virgil Davis, *The Bones Poems*
Jeffrey DeLotto, *Voices Writ in Sand*
Chris Ellery, *Elder Tree*
Dede Fox, *On Wings of Silence*
Alan Gann, *That's Entertainment*
Larry Griffin, *Cedar Plums*
Katherine Hoerth, *Goddess Wears Cowboy Boots*
Michael Jennings, *Crossings, a Record of Travel*
Betsy Joseph, *Only So Many Autumns*
Lynn Hoggard, *Motherland*
Gretchen Johnson, *A Trip Through Downer, Minnesota*
Ulf Kirchdorfer, *Chewing Green Leaves*
Laozi, *Daodejing*, tr. By David Breeden, Steven Schroeder, and Wally Swist
Janet McCann, *The Crone at the Casino*
Erin Murphy, *Ancilla*
Laurence Musgrove, *Local Bird*
Benjamin Myers, *Black Sunday*
Godspower Oboido, *Wandering Feet on Pebbled Shores*
Dave Oliphant, *The Pilgrimage, Selected Poems: 1962-2012*
Kornelijus Platelis, *Solitary Architectures*
Carol Coffee Reposa, *Underground Musicians*
Jan Seale, *The Parkinson Poems*
Steven Schroeder, *the moon, not the finger, pointing*
Glen Sorestad *Hazards of Eden*
Vincent Spina, *The Sumptuous Hills of Gulfport*
W.K. Stratton, *Ranchero Ford/ Dying in Red Dirt Country*
Gary Swaim, *Quixotic Notions*
Wally Swist, *Invocation*
Waldman, Ken, *Sports Page*
Loretta Diane Walker, *Ode to My Mother's Voice*
Dan Williams, *Past Purgatory, a Distant Paradise*
Jonas Zdanys, *The Angled Road*
Jonas Zdanys (ed.), *Pushing the Envelope, Epistolary Poems*
Jonas Zdanys, *Red Stones*
Jonas Zdanys, *Three White Horses*

For information on these and other Lamar University Literary Press books go to https://www.lamar.edu/literary-press/index.html

Acknowledgments

I am grateful to the editors of the following publications who have published some of the poems in this volume.

Adam, Eve, and the Riders of the Apocalypse
Animal Tales
Blue Hole
Book of the Year (Poetry Society of Texas)
Encore (National Federation of State Poetry Societies)
House of Poetry (Baylor University)
Ilya's Honey
Poetry at Round Top
Public Poetry (Houston)
Red River Review
Sea Dog Studios
Texas Poetry Calendar
Waco Wordfest Anthology
The Windhover

Thank you to
     my poetry-sharing partners: Susan Maxwell Campbell, Kathleen Hart, Jill Horner, and Janet McCann for their camaraderie and spot-on critiques.
     the Christ Church Writing Group of Temple TX (Donna Bowling, Jane DeBord, Jane Haywood, Jean Kubala, Susan Lanford, Mike McNamara, Les Minor, Tom Norman, Ron Owens, and Charlie Stoner) who, for more than 10 years have been the audience I have in mind when I sit down to write, and to the group's founder, Pruitt Davis, for his inspiration and criticism.
     the women's writing group, Stories to Tell, and their leader, Laura Jo Fojtasek, who have kept me writing for more than 12 years.
     the members of Poetry Society of Texas for opportunities and encouragement—especially to Anne McCrady.
     Carl Dennis for his book, "Poetry as Persuasion."
     the 1950's English teachers at P.S. 54 and Bennett High School in Buffalo, New York, for insisting I memorize all of those poems.
     the good folks at Lamar University Literary Press for their warmth and expertise.

An aged man is but a paltry thing,
A tattered coat upon a stick, unless
Soul clap hands and sing, and louder sing
For every tatter in its mortal dress.
                    —William Butler Yeats, "Sailing to Byzantium"

CONTENTS

An Aged Man Is But a Paltry Thing

A Tattered Coat upon a Stick

Unless

An Aged Man Is But a Paltry Thing

The Mask—An African Retrospective

Hewed from the oil nut tree
(The adz sticky with sap),
I was shaped by a master who
had as his praise name, oriki,
"He wielded his knife like a whisk."

Then the Society bathed me,
rubbed medicines into my crest,
and danced me into the market
throughout that long year of the plagues,
convinced they'd appeased the Mothers
when my bearer's train was the longest,
coin showers saluted his steps,
and singers repeatedly praised the sway
of my wooden bustle and breasts.

The sickness fled at my coming.
Yam harvest began to increase.
Our women gave birth to ibeji.
I strengthened our tribe's grizzled chief.
Year after year, after sunset,
drums vaunted my names to the town.

When my visage cracked, I was sent
to a place in our sacred shrine,
to be tended as town rites demand.
Then they forgot to anoint me.
My features were scoured by ants.

When trouble *next* plagued the tribe,
they chose to sell off their gods:
we were contraband slipped across borders,
crated together by dozens,
and chalked with catalog numbers.

I stand now with pinch-eyed relics,
stolen (it's thought) from Zaire,
while docents point out to children
The only thing known of my past:
"Carved from a single piece of wood."

Reflections

1. Aging

The first physical blow
from which, broken,
you are slow to recover:
a crack, a pause, then the earth slews;
a breath of life force whispers out,
and then another.

2. Pentimento

When I dust the mirrors, she comes to me,
that old crone, that blighted tree.
A web crinkles around her eyes.
Her blistered bark's a harsh surprise.
And though my thoughts, my acts, my voice,
still argue my wit, my strength, and poise,
she apes me dimly from the glass,
and makes me wonder when she'll pass
to my side, turn, and look at me,
imprisoned reflection of used to be.

3. Self-Regard

I made a frame for my life
Against things I shouldn't woo,
Rivers I should never cross,
Keyholes I must not snoop through.

When I had squared my quadrant,
Braced it against opposing views,
I gilded it with hubris
And let the dust accrue.

Yet, can any frame withstand
The losses that leave one reeling,
Or time, or obligations?
Now the gilt is peeling.

With Time

"The mind that is wise mourns less for what age takes away
than for what it leaves behind."
    —William Wordsworth

I was on a visit to the home place,
sleeping with my kids in my mother's room,
until a noise awoke me in the night.
Reassured that it was not my babies
needing me, I rose to get some water.
Know that this house, was vast and creepy,
with long hallways of uncarpeted oak floors.
My old folks all had died in its gray rooms.

Although not a woman to fancy haunts,
I was convinced I saw one in the dark.
There was, as required for such sightings,
a pane with moonlight leaking bleakly in,
and just inches from my nose, wild eyes glared
in a horrid face.

It looked to be a snake-less Gorgon's head
or that famous portrait by Giorgione
in which Time creates a ghastly crone.
"Who are you?" I sobbed, breathing out my shock,
but *sotto voce,* not to scare my boys.
"Just tell me who you are," I begged, this time
stretching my hand to touch an icy mirror.

"You'll think that's just the sort of symbolic
hoo-ha an art history major might
conjure up," I say defensively when
pressed to tell this story. I only know,
though that night happened forty years ago,
I pose the same question to my own mirror
every day. For I was scared by what
approached me in the glass: the idea
that, with time, I might become that thing.

Fishing Above the Bridge of My Nose

Thoughts like trout once darted and winked
in a tumbled golden patter;
roiled my brain with every leap,
snapped at words, grew sleek and fatter,
sliced beneath concepts, rose again,
amazed the sun with their spatter.

Now, a few slip sullen, slowly, deep
through murky bottom matter;
grope around a sunken hope,
no longer sky-bound gadders,
scarcely able to brush aside
life's formless, algaed tatters.

I'd hoped to snare one to feed our chatter,
but my net is frayed.

Why do I natter?

Luke 12:18

I called on a friend to deliver
some banana-bread words,
packaged small loaves of "Sorry."
I would rather have brought denial, distraction,
but I deliberately mentioned her cancer,
as the best books on grief advise.
She said, "It's out, you know."

"Yes, I know." I said it lightly,
thinking she meant over and done with,
then, realized she was saying *loose*,
loose in the sleek-minded, elegant body
that stands and kneels and says "Amen"
several pews ahead of me, in church, each Sunday.
And I said, "I know," again.

At once, everything is loose.
She is dying, as she always was,
as I am with the others in the pews,
only, perhaps, a little faster.
But a plank has been ripped from that
bigger barn that I ignored my Bible's caution
not to build. Small grain trickles out.

Now, the gentle machine of parish concerns
comforts her with soup, and cards, and hearty prayer;
and I would scoop a handful of kernels
from the vast and almost empty granary of faith,
which I, of course, have always meant to fill,
to bake a loaf of Communion Bread
on which we both, on which we all, might feed.

The Blind Artist

Today there is a blur where dearest faces were.
My eyes meander halls of infinite twilight,
They cannot trace the blue-backed soaring of the kite,
Nor track the bees that bumble lavender larkspur.
I can but dream of lapis, ruby, malachite.
Once known for sharp perception, I must now infer.
Today there is a blur where the dearest faces were.
My eyes meander halls of infinite twilight.
I am no longer hailed as premier connoisseur
Of radiance: sea sparkle, starred skies, and fires bright.
Vision, I have learned, was a revocable birthright.
I'm left with nothing other than this cri du coeur:
Today there is a blur where the dearest faces were.

Knight Errant

A plaint by one of several stone effigies in the
garden of a museum at Colmar, France

Oh, Lord, across the courtyard, on your cross,
You, who cured lepers, mended sinew, bone,
heal our poor noses eaten up by rain,
and save us from the curse of being stone!

Through museum windows, other statues
of your martyrs, carved in billowing wood,
raise stigmata, worm-wrought, to the eyes
of the yet-fleshed who pause before the rood.

Only St. Cecelia stands unmarred.
Her face is still enameled with her trust.
Even her body seems impervious
to any sign of Time's erratic lust.

Why is her figure spared, while the dulled blade
of her tormentor is eaten up in rust?
Why have hers, alone of our earthly woes,
been transubstantiated, turned to dust?

Dumbstruck

"How Will I Know This Is So?"
            —*Luke 1:18 (b) NRSV*

Zechariah, tending fires of incense,
You're frightened by Gabriel's sudden visit.
Good News is not always welcome is it?
Who sent this word? Does it make any sense?
Should you say, "Welcome," or prepare your defense?
Are you touched by God? Have you lost your wit?
Aged priest tending the fires of incense,
You mistrust the angel's sudden visit,
Counting pledges of answered prayer nonsense
For an old man, an old woman, neither fit.
You temporize, reluctant to submit.
I, too, inquire, "What's the evidence?"
Though I stoke altar fires with sweet incense.

Memory

"And then the lighting of the lamps. . ."
                —T.S. Eliot

All my memories live in a town
where twilight fades to night, in houses set
by river roads or high among the hills.
I prowl each peeling window ledge hoping
for a glimpse inside, the resolution
of shadows into a moment from my past,

until the lighting of an antique lamp,
a fire's kindling, echoed in a silver bowl,
or the flare of a lighter illumines
a precious face ripe with suggestions
of what truly happened. The light winks and is gone.
I am left outside the pane, yowling.

Was that a sneer I saw? A frown, a smile?
Who first named the sorrow, raised the fist?
Who sat in the gloom beyond the struck match?
Who was betrayed, and by whom? At whose feet the fault?
Now, seeing only my own faint reflection,
I raise a paw, to beat against the glass.

Crone Calling

"When an old man begged for food. . .the rabbit offered its own body, throwing itself into a fire the man had built. . .the old man. . .touched by the rabbit's virtue, drew the likeness of the rabbit on the Moon for all to see."

—Rabbit in the Moon, Wikipedia

Last night I missed my chance to see a blood-
red moon. When its wan light washed my chamber
and woke me from a dream, I burrowed deeper,
did not attend its progress through the sky.
Nature no longer has a hold on me
that would inspire a stumble out of doors.

Of late I've had encounters with other moons,
whose mellow clamor bled into the sky,
and have barely stopped myself from saying
a most dismissive, "So?" A red moon might
appear again on some more restless night
as, in the long-past years of maidenhood,
blue moons once did, and move me to fresh awe.

But the moon no longer plots the course I steer,
nor marks my path. Now, if I do look up,
it is to seek the rabbit, not the jocund face,
in moon's pearly cabochon, to listen for
a call to other mysteries than romance.

To the Pieces of the Second Last Baccarat Flute

I swear, I had barely grazed your delicate rim
when I heard your fragments rattle in the sink,
leaving me holding just your ornate stem.
How I delighted in those cut-glass
diamond designs, sixty years ago,
unfurling tissue from each fragile piece,
conscious of a new vocabulary
through which I heard myself
becoming householder, grown-up:
stemware, tumbler, goblet, flute.

The day after the wedding
I counted a dozen each
from parents' generous friends,
a zenith of hospitality potential
for a pair too shy to invite in-laws for lunch,
service for twelve, in a three-room upstairs flat.
Our kitchen table, draped
in oil cloth, accommodated four.

Through the years the feckless hands,
of children, maids, and guests,
diminished the crystal trove
in proportion as our fortunes rose.
A flute fell from a balcony,
scattering celebratory drops amid its shards.
Pure rage smashed a tumbler full of Maker's Mark.

In a moment of balance,
between want and greed, sometime in the '90s,
a table swathed in damask, with sterling service for eight,
held three brimming glasses at each place.
Since then, daughters have married,
bearing away four of this, or six of that.

The leaves that broadened the welcome
of the ebony table on every holiday
now stand in the basement under wraps.
 Just last year, three glasses fell from shaky fingers,
that were not mine, onto tile floors.

Tonight I fetched down the last two flutes
to let their angles catch the candlelight
once more. Then that tap against the rim,
and your shatter sparkled in the sink,
declaring there will be one less thing to pack
when the movers come tomorrow.

On Leaving Cyrano

"And I die without telling you! No more/ Shall my eyes
drink the sight of you like wine,/ Never more with
a look that is a kiss,/ Follow the sweet grace of you. . . "
—Edmond Rostand, *Cyrano de Bergerac*

The play, more enthusiasm than craft,
got off to a slow start that night.
No matter. We find as much pleasure,
as a rule, in effort as in flight.
Cyrano was poignant on the topic of his nose.
Rosalind's grace, as always, a delight.
Rostand's wit propelled their story.
Stage direction evoked their tragic plight.

So why, at intermission, did we stand,
share a glance, then move into the night?
The ride back home would take an hour.
It hurt our backs to sit upright.
The dog had not had dinner,
but we didn't mean to slight
the players and their earnestness,
or the centuries-gone playwright.

By the time we reached the car
we were feeling quite contrite.
"We've never walked out of a play before!"
"How thoroughly impolite!"
"We shouldn't have left the theater."
"That simply wasn't right."

The chance of seeing *Cyrano* again
is surely rather slight.
In fact, the time left for theater-going,
at our age, is, I suspect, finite.
If we try to conjure plays from decades past,
our memories fade to a pale lime-light.
But that evening we couldn't bear—

it's time to be forthright—
to sit with Rosalind and Cyrano
and feel our hearts grow tight,
to watch each leaving someone loved,
their tears so bitter-bright.

The Chambered Nautilus

A response to Oliver Wendell Holmes, Sr.

I pivoted 'round my own past places,
exquisite, sealed off, left behind.
My eyes upon their eager stalks
were tiny pin holes so purblind,

that I was unable to admire
the chambered splendor I'd unwind
from both cracked crab and carrion,
on which, indifferently, I dined.

(As predator and sarcovore,
my radial glory I defined.)
Around my mouth were processes
of lengthy tentacles, entwined,

that shoveled in sea-slime and sludge
until my shell was pearly-lined.
Through the milky quarters where, I
imagined, beauty was outlined,

I siphoned up salt water, air,
my own elixir, quite sublime.
I dove to scavenge bottom filth,
as I grew yet more hyaline.

Condemned by tenderness of flesh
(for which I blamed God's bent design),
I built my shell. Then, rotting loose,
I left it as a tide-beached rind,

and polished nacre on a shelf,
it soon became an esthete's shrine.
Now, through the passing of the years
my emptied carcass will still shine.

Equipoise: *Mark, Andrew, Camela, 2015*

The three portraits are balanced on one gray wall.
Within black frames, white mats, clear-eyed faces
gaze in unison, across the gallery.
Similarly calm demeanors, muted restraint, suggest relationship.
Three siblings? A father and his children?
Two parents and a son? Or three strangers
whom a common photographic technique has made one?

I place a chair at the intersection
of their gazes and sit, acknowledging,
whoever these people are, the artist
that captured their images, has bent them
to his will. These portraits were not "taken"
as Northerners might say. Rather, they were
"made" with artistic deliberation.

The hand of the photographer is here.
Though absent the trappings of opulence,
his aesthetic speaks of the Renaissance,
a style with which an artist might paint
doge or duchess to indicate their power:
among the three, the only trinket, a pearled heart,
small and lost, at Camela's mottled neck.

Each subject is backed by a horizon
barely hinted at: a twilight forest,
a sunset harbor, a darkening shore.
The sitters' clothes extend the metaphor:
a loose shirt, collarless sweater, white tee.
Their hair, features, are unadorned, timeless.
Forthright self-possession keeps their secrets.

As I stare at them, try to winkle out
their thoughts, I feel them inclining toward me.
I intuit, "Life's not what I thought it would be."
I discern, "How bravely can I face my aging?"
I descry, "I've always done what was asked of me."
Then I realize the words I read in their faces
might well be those they see etched upon my own.

My Last Pictures

"To be without some of the things you want is
 an indispensable part of happiness."
                —Bertrand Russell

One thing I knew,
even before the market bubble burst,
I would never buy another painting;
never prowl gallery or street fair
with the tip-toe expectation
that I might meet a mirror
or window
that I couldn't live without,
an object that would tell
me and my neighbors
who and where I was.

My walls were full
with no more room for pictures.
I could never shroud
the painted post cards
of my yesterdays,
place them in the attic
to make way for a newer find.
 My pocket book was empty,
and I was seventy-five—
could reckon just a few tomorrows.
I needed to rest with what I knew.

It was. . . acceptable. . .
this understanding
that, in yet another area of life,
options had been curtailed,
because past choices had been good ones,
with comfortable consequences.

And then I saw her work:
shop windows blazed
with books and flowers.

Sunshine danced on awnings.
Interiors, rich in fruit
and bulging furniture,
shone with the beauty
of having seen better days.
An atelier with prints strung
on a sagging wire was candent
with the holy light
of promise and precision.
Her houses and street corners
with indeterminate eyes—
closed up and inviting
all at once—were places
I had always meant to see,
and was sure that I had left
not an hour before,
twilit corners that mirrored my life,
squared-off spaces that looked out
and remembered me.

I could say they were nothing
but smears on canvas:
there amid the browns
a stroke of white,
the yellow patch that marked a
lampshade or an awning,
a joyous suffusion of pink;
but taken together they declared
just how long since
I had felt the itch
to acquire, to look long enough
at anything
to claim it as my own.

I am on a different path now,
trying to have done with having.
Still, for a moment,
in the framed dimensions
of this white page,
I can let those pictures go
and keep them too.

Parent's Directive

If, after a stroke, I am hateful,
punching the attendant, who tells me what to wear
(the clean robe, not the dirty one),
who tries to brush my tangled hair;

if, after a stroke, I am hateful,
snarling "You sold my Lladro. Don't you even care?
The Chippendale! the Waterford!
No, you don't ever play me fair;"

if after a stroke, I am hateful,
biting your kind fingers that feed me Camembert
or fresh grapes from the market place;
if I blight grandkids with my STARE;

remember how you loved me once.
Forgive my ravening despair.

Euthanasia

A feathered V has crashed to earth
and lies odd-angled, limp, denied,
a scarcely breathing, ruptured flight
with dim and pearly eye.

The thing to do, my son decides,
is still, at once, its faltering cry.
He sends me indoors with his child,
who poses frightened questions: "Why?"

The spade we keep beside the shed
he takes to crush and nullify
with one commiserating stroke
the night hawk's memory of the sky.

On broken wings, bird tries to rise.
Again. Again. It won't abide
the death delivered by a hand
that only wants to dignify.

Again, again, we hear the blows
through curtained windows, closed inside.
"What is it? What is Daddy doing?"
"He's helping that poor creature die."

Once he has finished, buried it,
he rubs his fevered face and cries,
washes his hands and holds his child,
and forbears to tell him lies.

Regrets

1. The Declamation Piece

(After John McCrae)

I was too young, just yet, to know
What it meant for poppies to blow,
That rhythmic sounds could beautify
Phrases that ought to horrify,
That men who murder are called "foe,"

That crosses warn, "Corpses below,"
That blood meal makes the poppies grow,
That "Dead" connotes muck, stench, blowfly.
I was too young

To reckon what the widows know,
Ignominies veterans undergo:
The pinned up sleeve, the midnight cry,
Zealous parades that feed the lie.
I read the poem with brio, though.
I was too young.

2. Tears or Teeth

"The baby has known the dragon intimately ever
since he had an imagination. What the fairy tale
provides for him is a St. George to kill the dragon."
            —G.K. Chesterton

I never wanted my sons to think
the world is truly a scary place.
I scorned parents who would watch with a wink
as terror spread over their child's face
when they read of cruel witches, wolves that slink,
or piglets who vanish without a trace.

My readings tuned heartstrings, pliant and pink,
so that, when tugged, they responded with grace.
I never wanted my sons to think
the world was truly a scary place.

I never read them the fanciful tales
by Perrault, Jacobs, or the Brothers Grimm.
I only read those where heroes were frail,
where one's three wishes would rarely avail,
and Andersen gloom was wont to prevail:
"Now, Boys, can you say 'Human Condition?'"
My children are grown; have made their own worlds,
but I have wondered in the interim,
did I daunt them more with those crybaby tales
than had I read Jacobs, Perrault, or Grimm?

3.   Meeting Places

A meeting place may be the image on a painter's canvas
of a red brick house in Bruges,
one he composed from all his walks
around the city: the roof of this dwelling,
the chimney pot of that, a sun-dazzled bow window,
in whose forecourt real people garden, sew, and play,
that leaves the critics, over the centuries, worrying
their Van Dykes or soul patches, trying to guess, "Where?"

or a church whose varnished pews
à la *Places in the Heart*
hold people who have never met
and those long lost to one another
in a conversation that includes each and every saint.
They slip in from their cloud contemplation, their plows,
their ergonomic chairs, to pass the peace and sacred bread,
to know each other as God's children, to ask and offer pardon;

or the chamber inside my head
where feeble will and best intentions swirl,
always planning to write the sonnet,

bake the bread, or call the friend,
and where somehow I find that I am able to hold
such dreams in such a way that they shine as if completed;
and I see myself as more of a person and in a better place
than I have any right to be.

4. The Bats

When I first retired, those last months
before Betsy died, Two Thousand Five,
or so, I had a job taking tourists
through the Meramac Caves in Missouri.
I worked the morning shift, all that summer.

On every single tour I always paused
before the great maw where the bats fly out
each evening. I tried to make folks imagine
the dark screech-soaked scarf
they could see for themselves,
if they came back on the Twilight Tour.

I numbered the bodies
that would hurtle through the dusk.
"Millions," I said.
Of course, millions barely begins to hint
at the sensation of standing by
while that frantic arc lifts from the darkness,
bends left, dissipates in the pale gray sky.
So why insist on this didactic pause
just as I began each morning's hike?

Only because it's a bit easier
for someone to believe in the hidden bats
before he is beguiled by the sights below.
Folks think of bats as denizens of the dark,
creatures that should soar from a space
as sightless as the breath being exhaled
from the orifice at whose entrance we stood

while the group listened to my patter
over the liquid echoes of dripstone.

If sight-seers credit the presence of bats
when they file down rusted metal stairs,
not liking the nasty feel of the rail,
they might not forget them all together
as I trip the switch to light the first cavern
and set before them drapes, folds, chandeliers—
calcite concatenations of kitsch–like those
that flaunt themselves in every commercial cave.

Once in spot-lit areas of the caves,
visitors too easily set their minds to work
projecting Rorschachs on the rocks,
heedless that, snug above them, their tiny
raw faces folded into scaly wings,
the bats are still digesting insect prey
gorged last night at eventide.

When Betsy and I were young—when
we were raising our children—we tried
to make them pause before the mouths
of caves to hear about the bats inside.
I don't recall that they ever listened.

The Docent at Laguna Gloria

When Clara Driscoll's husband built her
a villa in Nineteen-Sixteen,
she hung a bell to toll the hours,
chose "Time" for the gardens' theme,
placed a dial to mark the passage
of the fiery Texas sun
and imported Roman statues,
to declare the seasons one by one.

When have gardens *ever* required
such a heavy-handed device?
To remind us that time is fleeing,
surely, Nature's offerings suffice.
The passage of both day and season
is reckoned in bird song, falling leaves.
A garden needs no furnishings
but benches where guests might take their ease.

Despite honors accorded him,
Time has treated these gardens ill.
From his pawing depredations
the bell's been tarnished, its throat is still.
The sundial, overcome with vines,
has been tumbled and lies broken.
Fountains that burbled ballads once
are emptied now, their poems unspoken.

The four statues on their plinths
have suffered Time and come to grief.
Winter huddles in soot-smeared cloaks.
A falling branch chipped Flora's wreath.
The crumbling of Summer's basket
revealed her rusty armature.
The shock of wheat that Fall embraces
is marred by stains of roosting birds.

Though Clara thought to capture him,
end his ravenous pacing to and fro,

to stay his gnawing, black decay,
as she had done at the Alamo,
by inviting him into her gardens, and
allowing his brute force free range,
today, beneath her oaks, we see
Time's wolfish hunger is never assuaged.

Notre Dame de Paris

When monuments catch fire, as I did,
in a country of much ceremony,
little faith, that counts on tourist ardor
to hallow and revivify old stones,
to embrocate with reverent fingers
the paraphernalia of lost awe,

when lead that holds old glass begins to melt,
and my flèche, a fire brand collapsing,
puts paid to oaken timbers from ancient trees,
and as Le Stryge looks on with mocking eyes,
I remind myself that I'm the fifth church
in this place, and that kings have come and gone.

As unbelieving men, in disbelief,
gather in the courtyard promising repair,
no matter what the cost, to those whose cameras,
phones, spread my shame throughout the screenosphere,
and les Gilets Jaunes prepare responses
to such outrage with placards and with fists,

I recall the last time I was defiled,
made a temple to The Reasonable
(strange how men always worship what they aren't).
Now, as they crawl through me, tap on cooling stone,
as I wait to see what will happen next,
sighs slip through my organ's eight hundred pipes.

Death of a Poet

"I shall die in Paris. . ."
                    —César Vallejo

I shall die here in Texas while sleet is flinging
against the windows of an northern house where I,
as a child, wrote lines that both alarmed and soothed me.

Trees in that winter world will moil and moan my loss
though my current clime may offer no more than mist,
the abrupt cough of a crow, to mark my passing.

The binder on my desk will await my return,
its crabbed and cryptic notations eager to be
taken up, read, made into the poems first promised

when my thoughts overwhelmed me and I scrawled them down
to be pondered and embroidered another day
(a perhaps that will not happen now, or ever):

an assessment of the capacitance of love;
the need for people to be both seen and seen to;
the "smear of suffering" I'd planned to vivify

in verse; the wounds that gimme and gotcha impose;
the plaint that dying wasn't what I feared, but this:
the awful in-between before it comes to pass;

poems I had hoped to title, "O Brightening Glance,"
"Then Perhaps Because of the Rain," "Mise in Abîme,"
"On Maple Branches Broken in the Autumn Snows,"

all the someday verses that swirled inside of me,
until I became uncomfortable with wonder
and, then, decided I had written my last poem.

"What's New, Old Cat?"

Max regards me with one drowsy eye.
His answer, "Nothing," hangs in the air.
What novelty could excite his notice?
His indifference is doctrinaire.

Now, roused by my day's-end appearance,
he stretches, flexes claws, limbers joints.
He's too indolent even to greet me,
his go-to mantra being, "What's the point?"

Max came to me already jaded
by life lived on the meanest of streets:
his scarred flanks proclaiming his valor,
his flaccid belly mistrusting of treats.

Though coaxed through my door, into my world,
after long campaigns of hide and peek,
he still slinks off to his low-life haunts,
severing communication for weeks.

As I lift him on to my needy lap,
I expect momentary defense
before his assenting burr begins,
or whatever grace he deigns to dispense.

I give him news of my weekday world:
family discussions that went awry,
the lunch that ended in a betrayal,
my trip to the wash room for a good cry.

His purring declares what I should have learned
by now, but, stubbornly, haven't done:
whatever my misfortune, anguish,
loss, there is nothing new under the sun.

Dark Time

"This is the dark time, my love . . .
It is the man of death, my love, the strange invader
watching you sleep and aiming at your dream."
                    —Martin Carter.

True, the night is a wall of black
Pressed against the curtained window,
Muffling the whine of the wind
In the ancient, unputtied, pane.

But why can't you rest, accepting
This owl-felted in between?
Why the thrashing toward a morning
That you surely know will be filled

With an even greater darkness?
Your concerns unlock this chamber
Meant to protect us from the night.
Enumeration of evils

Is not erasure. Even less
Is it control. Now a cipher
Of light, be it moon's or morning's,
Begins to pierce the icy pane.

The only silhouette I see
Watching beside my bed is yours.

Talking It Out

There you go blundering your clumsy "Whys?"
baring doubts that, once, you would not have condoned,
ransacking heaven and earth for reasons.
For my sake, please, leave the questions alone.

You, a person I thought competent, wise,
worry your Bible, a dog with its bone,
lament your Lord's unbearable treason,
ask why He has swapped your bread for a stone.

I live with your pain, have heard your night-cries,
your piteous monologues, drone upon drone.
You once advised, "All things have their seasons."
Now that you suffer, perspective has flown.

Again your afflictions you re-itemize.
I, too, am broken, undone, and alone.
You, who gave hope, are now lost to reason,
who were my lode star, are now my millstone.

Youth and Then

After reading Noailles's "La Jeunesse"

O, joyous, ardent, springtime of life,
Garlands of promise sift from your hands.
All that we are to mean or to be
Seems determined by years spent in your lands.

Some cross your fields, and the sparrow's flight
Makes more of a sign on the dazzled grass
(No matter how bright or fraught their lives)
Than the pathways they mark as they pass.

Others, their eyes green as budded leaves,
Establish their brands again and again,
Determined that they be seen by all
Before they're expelled from life's playpen.

When, in the end, all reach middle age,
The underachieved may turn to shouting
(Now fearful that life has passed them by),
While the over-achieved start self-doubting.

Some whisper their way toward the end of life.
Some furnish their cars with vanity plates.
But once Age has gripped our sagging necks
Everyone's volume moderates.

Ab Astra

I have determined I will avoid
any thoughts of the far-flung skies,
or the icy ardor of the stars,

or the vast empty that surrounds each
flaming ball, and makes as nothing
the chills and fevers of my small life.

How well I understand ancient man
who strove to defy vacantness
by connecting blazing astral dots,

and imposing faces of his gods
upon the over-arching bleak.
But my defense is even surer:

By dallying in dailiness, I
am spared a confrontation with
queries for which I have no answers.

I focus on human tedium
and find the hummings of the hive
drown the anxious echoes of the spheres.

Postcard

Greetings from the Land of the Way Things Are.
A family confab has brought me today
to the house of a well-intentioned child.

The blaze of candles that you watched me
extinguish at that last birthday party
suggests I may never be allowed to leave here.

No wonder the sky whimpered as it did
each aching mile on the long road to this place.
Everything has been anticipated to ease

my transition. But my small belongings,
disposed as they are about this room,
look as out of place as I feel in this new life.

The chickens' evening mutter that seeps
through the windows open to the breeze,
provokes yearning for the squalls of city streets.

The new daughter-in-law, with her unknown ways,
unfolds a comforter on the narrow bed,
does not mention the life for two she'd hoped to have.

In the dark I refuse to whine. I grope for memories
left behind, clasp the small hope of a someday return
to now untended rooms of memory and identity,
home.

Prayer

"... for we do not know how to pray as we ought, But that very Spirit intercedes for us..."
—Romans 8:26 (b) NRSV

Today is Tuesday,
and I am praying for
the relative of my friend,
whichever friend it was
who asked me to pray,
this morning, for this person.
And I remember distinctly
that I asked What's-Her-Name
for the name of this relative,
or perhaps it was a friend,
but, of course, by now,
I have forgotten that name, as well
as that of my friend;

And I have also forgotten
the nature of the trial
this person will undergo today.
So just to be on the safe side,
I pray for all beings in Your creation
who face challenges today.
May they draw strength
from the knowledge
of Your caring presence.
Please hear my prayer,
and in case I have the day wrong,
please remember my prayer
tomorrow.

A tattered coat upon a stick

Weekends in Hammondsport

It seemed every trip was the same: riding
into the reluctant Friday evening
after my father got off work; stopping once
so he could fill up the Nash at a station
whose lone pump bore a glowing red and white crown,
then on again into the thickening dark;

at last, stumbling along a gravel path
toward a dim porch light and two unwelcomed hugs,
one of them whiskered, the other whiskery;
climbing the creaking stairs to the attic room,
with the calendar picture of the Dionne
Quintuplets above the lumpy, twanging bed;

remembering, as Mother heard my prayers,
that one of those for whom I asked a blessing
this night, though never in my prayers at home,
had hung the picture of five well-behaved girls,
in pastel dresses, dancing in a meadow,
and that she was the Grandma who often said
her pack of stepchildren would have driven her mad
were it not for the whip she kept at the ready,
both morning and night, just beside the back door.

Proving Up the Land

In his last days Grandfather often spoke
of years homesteading in Saskatchewan,
and his efforts at "proving up the land."

The quaint phrase made no sense to me at first.
Something he was obliged to justify?
Or was "prove" just "improve" in his country talk?

I've since learned the government required both:
to earn his allotted homestead acres,
he had to build a cabin and live there,

then break the soil with his plow, and sow.
The crops of wheat and children, seeded, raised,
were the improvements homesteading required.

Once his compliance had been witnessed to,
by his few neighbors on the vast brown plain,
he might say the land had been "proved up," was his.

I see him, with reins around his shoulders,
walking in straight rows, behind his oxen,
as the plowshare curled the sod between them;

counting acres of broken and worked land;
tallying the blisters on his hands and feet;
proving up himself as a man of worth.

His wife was left to doctor the disasters
bound to happen to six kids in one room
with little food, no space, and open fires.

What standards would measure her proving up?
Her unwearied recitations of love
for the smelly, restless little bodies in her charge?

The chaos that she coped with every day?
Scriptures read to her children by the fire's light?
The six years they were sent unshod to school?

Patient patching of ragged hand-me-downs?
The bucket of rendered lard left to cool
that scalded her toddler's pink and precious face?

Was her family's proving up confirmed
when, though she succumbed to "female problems,"
each member of her little brood survived?

Or would she have lost the right to make a claim
when her second youngest, shown her photo
on his twelfth birthday, didn't know who she was?

The last time I saw grandfather, he spoke
of children who were sent away on trains,
aunts' addresses on tags around their necks;

the emptied cabin, sale of plow and oxen;
a rough sandstone marker inscribed "Mother,"
the sole improvement left upon his land.

Bleeding Hearts

The bleeding hearts are stitched with fuchsia jewels
above swatches of ornamental grass,
but they're ripping out Mrs. Larson's garden
to make way for the Humboldt underpass.

The bleeding hearts are stitched with fuchsia jewels,
the lilies of the valley almost spent.
The fence was offered, curbside, for kindling.
Now mixers are churning with fresh cement.

Above swatches of ornamental grass,
patches of iris, portulaca, chive,
she looks out from her shadowed porch to see
wheelbarrows of rocks trundled down the drive.

Neighbors admired Mrs. Larson's garden.
People stopped to chat about her flowers,
saw her with bonnet, trowel, and kneeling pad,
radiant in early morning hours.

Of course we need the Humboldt underpass
more than dahlia beds, geranium pots,
more than one woman's dreams and peonies,
or graveled walks hemmed with forget-me-nots.

The Peasant in the Blue Smock

A painting by Paul Cezanne

I have seen that look before:
in my great-grandfather's eyes
when he spoke about the old country,
remembered the wife he'd lost there.

He, too, was a working man,
a weaver who spent his days
crawling atop the giant looms
to oil or adjust a pulley,

below to rethread heddles—
as lost to his craft as Cezanne's man
who is dressed in his paint-splashed smock,
his hands, also, battered by his work.

Only sometimes, evenings
mostly, when I was dispatched
to fetch Grandpa home from the tavern,
after he'd had his pint and tot,
was that drawn look in his dark eyes.

Happy Holidays

Have you met my father-in-law?
A clamorous man, he's possessed
by a brace of ideas he bagged,
sometime in the mid Seventies,

about democracy and hair length,
and the consent of the governed.
He hung these, ankles up, and dripping,
on one wall of his draughty mind;

and still delights to display their stiff forms
to our captive Thanksgiving guests,
or to his great grandchildren, after
each takes a turn pulling his finger.

My wife can be seen drawing deep
cleansing breaths, in November.

Dry Dock

Her husband's old friends have sprung leaks,
and are foundering. When they moor
at the coffee shop once a week
their blistered hulls creak and snap.
As one sits down, he places his hands
together, presses them against his knees
to keep sly and sudden shivers
from running through his timbers.
Three raise cups to barnacled lips
(skin cancers are rife this year),
all mention which medical boat wrights
have had them in for needed repairs:
the caulking of a hold,
the tightening of a rudder,
the riveting of a boiler,
the stiffening of a mast.

At times, each is lost to the conversation
by desperate thoughts of his own faulty keel
—the argot he has learned to describe it,
gleaned from technicians who solder and scrape—
and does not listen to the others' recitations.
But the talk keeps going. Pennants snap.
Whether they have been trawlers or cruise ships
in their past lives, they have a yarn to spin.

They try to ignore the chill winds
flapping through furled sails and shrouds.
They regale one another
with brave words of high seas survived,
the idiocies of insurance,
the more modest of the symptoms
that threaten to scuttle them.
(The wormwood, they can't bear to name.)
They mock the storms they foresee,
forked lightning on the horizon.

At last, one by one, harried wives,
who still have driver's licenses,
 arrive to guide the old craft home.

Write What You Know

My grandmother, who attends all my meets,
is an unaggressive woman in every way.
She asks why it is I like to compete
(research for a character she plans to portray).

How could a staid old writer comprehend
swimming a mile, anchoring a relay:
the engulfing passion of moments when
the blurred line dissolves between work and play,
how the yearning suspense entices me
across the pool's charged tumult, day after day?

She could never enter the world of sport,
given her kindly, though advanced, decay.
I can make but one suggestion for her:
"Nana, why don't you write about croquet?"

Luke 23:42

"Remember your own Baptism," the preacher exhorts,
approaching the family at the font.
The sleeping child wakes, reddens, prepares to cry,
as his wispy curls are dampened in the name
of the Father, the Son, and the Holy Spirit.

My mother, in the pew beside me, cannot recall her Baptism,
for she, like this child, was blessed with sacramental waters
when she was a baby in her parents' arms.
But she also has no recollection that this gift
has been conferred upon her,

no memory of her confirmation
(of the leatherette Bible with the underlined verse,
her first pair of stockings and two-inch heels).
She does not carry in her occluded mind the wedding vows
(the blue dress, the wartime wildflower bouquet),
or the promises she made in this very space to raise
her own children (one laughed, the other cried,
as each, in turn, wore her yellowed Christening gown)
in the nurture and admonition of the Lord.

"I have a good memory," she says gamely. "It's just short."
She is lucky to remember that today is Sunday.
It seems it is her history, not her sin, being washed away.
And who is left to remember for her?
Only the daughters and grandkids who listened to stories
of her once-self when she was still able to tell them.
Yet here she stands with the rest of the congregation
to welcome this new child into our midst. And afterwards,
she will press her withered fingers to the baby's cheek
and tell his parents of his wondrous beauty.

Later in the service when the bread and wine are shared,
it is for her and others like her that I pray, "Jesus *they* can't,
so, remember *for* them when you come into your kingdom."

Not for Sissies

"Attention must be paid . . ."
                    —Arthur Miller, *Death of a Salesman*

They do not, as yet, consider these engagements
as treats, or outings, big events in their lives;
however, the visits and revisits
to Doctors for Chronic Conditions *are*
becoming more prominently featured
on their calendar: the smiling nurse,
who calls them by name, as few others now do;
the morning appointments, reserved for those,
like them, whose agendas are nearly blank;
the silent waiting rooms where old people
have even less to say than when they're dining out;
the slight tensing of the patient for whom
this meeting is scheduled
as the 15 minutes of attention approaches:

Must review the list I wrote
on this envelope flap. Hmmm. Must also
pay the bill that came last week in this same
envelope. Must ask about blood pressure,
the mole, the gastric distress, whatever
has caused me to wake at two a.m.
and do angry battle with my pillow.

Now they are directed to the exam room,
and another silent, vacant wait.
At last, each grips the doctor's soft, kind hand.
He might be able to ease the concern:
"As we get older . . . ," the discomfort: "Let's try this
drug/ treatment/ deprivation, for six weeks. . . ,"
the cost: "These samples will get you started . . . ,"
but the patient's hope is checked by petulance:

As if I am a motor that needs revving!
Why doesn't he admit, you can't fix old?

Meanwhile the spouse scribbles instructions
in a notebook so the other cannot argue later,
"I was there, and that is never what was said!"

What is the value of mornings spent in this way?
Is it the reassurances? Or the diminution—
however temporary—of the pain?
Or the moment when the well one, or, at least,
 the one whose frailing is not the subject
of today's examination, sets down
the note book and sees his wife/ her man
with refreshed eyes, *looks*—past aggravations,
and mirrored infirmities—at the stubborn
soul across the room, so mortal, so lost, and so dear.

Words to Live By

For our grandmother and great aunt

When they would say to us, "Go ben the hoose,"
we knew there had been enough shenanigans,
that the grownups wished to reclaim their space.
What we didn't know was that their house in Scotland
had only a butt and a ben: two rooms for a family of seven.

When they said we were "toosie-headed,"
we knew we were in for a firm-handed hair brushing.
Our finger curls would be remade, ribbons retied.
We didn't know the pleasure that this gave old hands
whose own head had been shaved on the crossing due to lice.

When they said, "Go on with ye," or "My eye,"
we knew they weren't buying the excuse we proposed
for whatever mischief we were up to.
We didn't know they thought they'd heard it all:
in Scotland, and in Canada, before coming to the States.

When they said, "I'll gi'ye the back of me hand,"
we knew that they were joking, because they adored us,
and we'd not been struck in our four and eight year old lives.
What we didn't know was they were brought up differently,
their cheeks reddened by their mother's admonitory slaps.

When they said, "For fun for your belly to make your taes laugh,"
we knew that "taes" were "toes," but we also knew that
Why questions we'd asked, eavesdropping on their conversation,
would not be answered. Grown-up subjects were not for us,
so we let ourselves be distracted by thoughts of laughing toes.

When they said "coos" instead of "cows," "cam" instead of "calm,"
said a thing was "bonny," we knew it was the old country talking,
and we smiled secretly at their antiquated ways.
We never wondered why some words were scrubbed of accent,
but those that remained inflected, seemed to harbor tears.

When they said, to each other, "Little pleases bairns,"
we knew they were laughing at themselves, or perhaps at us,
for being delighted by something uncomplicated, childlike.
We didn't know they also used that phrase to dismiss
aspects of the strange culture they saw around them.

On New Year's Eve, when each held a dram of whisky
and cried, "Long may your lum reek with other folks' coal,"
we knew both that "lum" meant chimney, and that they
were mocking themselves as tightfisted Scots, but not
that the words recalled Auld Reekie, the city they were from.

When one said, "Mind my toes" during our rough play,
or "Mind your fingers," when she taught us to cook and sew,
or "Mind your heart," when we grew to be young women,
we thought the words an odd caution. Then, visiting Scotland,
we saw a sign by a low doorway that said, "Mind your head."

When one said, "The glass fell away in me hand,"
we knew she was marveling that the deftness of her acts
had faltered, could no longer be a source of pride for her—
a woman who'd always been so quick witted, so clever—
but we didn't know we were already losing her.

To My Out-of-State Aunt Who Is Imploring Me to Visit Yet Again

Today, as yesterday, you choose
independence. You will, you vow,
never go to a "nursing home."
You spit the words as if they were
a curse.

But you called to say how lonely
life is. No one ever visits.
As the first winter storm rages,
you, once so compassionate, wonder
how it will affect,

not the millions menaced by it,
but only you. What will you do
when the lights go out? If I suggest
you have opted for freedom over
security,

you respond that one day I'll be
in your position and be backed
against the either/ors of age
having to make the same hopeless
choices.

Then, you promise me (as grimly
pleased as the thirteenth fairy
at Sleeping Beauty's christening),
then, even I will understand,
comprehend,

all that you struggle with today.
When my own life becomes unwieldy,
then, perhaps, I will think of you,
and will wish I'd come more often.
Of course, I will.

I don't know if you remember
the story of a long ago man
who gives his mother half a blanket,
sends her to the burial ground
alone?

He watches as his children learn,
from his example, to treat him
indifferently, when it is his turn
to walk away from the ardors
of this world.

Just outside their hut, his son rips up
a blanket: half for his father's time alone.
The younger man has learned the lesson:
Be stingy with the dying, for you can
never give enough.

Do I divide the blanket when
I beg you to be reasonable,
say you can't be safe at home,
that you, like everyone, need to face
"Reality?"

I would not withhold one thing
I could possibly give to you.
Yet when you need new strategies,
but want the world to be as it was,
no changes,

it is you who rend the blanket
in your tug-a-war with how things are.
I can only offer you the frayed piece
you seem to need the most. Dear one,
please take it.

Artist, Retrospective

The potter apologized.
It had been a short summer's sabbatical;
his only finished pieces,
five hoodoo-like ceramic fabrications—
what with packing up a life-time of work,
and preparing for his retirement.

hubris to have thought
myself Creator because
my hands could fashion things

Each stolid oversized form
was planted on a block of wood, its paired feet
framing a converging arch.
Here, a rakued pall met glazed and spiky life.
There, ruin, pressing like a dome,
caused tongues of clay to spring in all directions.

my mute offerings
beg, see me well, comprehend
the cost each time I make

In another piece, life wore
loss as a party hat and seemed to declare,
"I know it's not becoming.
It makes my face too long, but it's not seemly
to yank it off in public.
I will act the fool, await some privacy."

can you feel the song
I once hoped these shapes would sing
for all their woodenness

And then, facing each other,
two forms: lively death embracing deadly life.
He said they were reflections
on mortality. Here was youth unfolding;

there, the mature self, aging,
then shriveling to the point of its extinction.

how could I submit
such knowing to be affirmed
by the kiln's hectic heat

He'd slowly fingered the clay
to find the place where youth's flourishing halted
and age began its closing.
He'd tried to balance élan with acceptance
of Ending's grim abruptness
that makes each promise a hobbled irony.

spurning troubled truths
wishing they were otherwise
I have betrayed the work

Yet the thoughts, whose tails he'd grasped
so tightly, finally, had eluded him.
Rhythms, with which yielding might
have infused the clay, were blocked by his terror
at being helpless to stop
disruption of even the most joyous song.

I dallied, waiting
for challenges big enough
then found them all too great

Cooking Lessons

In the Nineteen Forties, "Let's write a cookbook"
was the Church-Lady version of MGM's "Hey, Kids!
Lets put on a show!" Such collections provided
broad opportunities for gastronomic talent to shine,
for seeing one's name in print and raising money—
for much debated good works—and also for playing
a little gotcha—by revealing just how much butter
actually went in to those family recipes, clucked
and oohed over at the monthly potluck suppers.

The little book I consult once a year
for the Thanksgiving "Baked Corn Casserole"
is permanently folded to Page Seven
which this recipe shares with one for "Fluffy Meat Loaf."
Staples have bled rustily into the paper,
greasy fingerprints have dimmed the instructions
(The best recipes are always on the stickiest pages.),
a stain of spilled coffee circles the ingredients.

"A pinch of" has been penciled beside the word "salt,"
the only clarification Mom was willing to give
in 1968, the first time I prepared this dish.
The passed-along book was almost 20 years old by then,
its pages yellowed. Most of the ladies
who had contributed recipes had yellowed by then,
as well, but still wore wide hats and kidskin gloves,
and were still called, Mrs. Richard Roath, Mrs. Frederick
Brock, their first names lost to etiquette of the day.

Fifty years on, I make this casserole
each November, but rarely inquire
what other delights "Presbyterians Cook"
might have offered for family feasts.
Today I finger the pages looking for the secrets
my mother shared with her friends. She, of course,
is gone, but here are her Molded Tuna Salad,
her One-egg Chocolate Cake, Ranger Cookies,
Viennese Tea Cakes, and Coconut Dreams.

Memories of her sweet tooth have outlived
her by a decade. Most of the recipes have no more
than eight ingredients. One calls for a 25-cent bag
of potato chips. Another requires both catsup
and Campbell's Crème of Mushroom Soup.

 Sponsoring ads that appear, intermingled
with table graces, are for fish markets, druggists,
Ben Franklin Five and Tens, the candy store
by my old elementary school, and a Main Street furrier.
And here are the old names of the ancient ladies,
young once, but not when I knew them: ladies
against whom the women in my immigrant family
measured the progress of their assimilation
into church and society: as one or another became
group chairman, president of the Women's Association,
first woman to be named deacon, elder, or trustee.

The almost forgotten ladies erupt from pages
hedged in by instructions for boiled dressings,
and many references to chipped beef and Velveeta.
 Here, women who abashed my grandmother,
irritated my no-nonsense mother, or sent my aunt
to the Ladies' Parlor in tears. There, a minister's wife
whose name was whispered with a kind of awe.
They are ladies who became caricatures for me
when outlined in my mother's mixture
of sharp-tongued humor, Christian forbearance,
 and uncanny psychological insight.
Most of them dead even longer than Mom—

petty triumphs, defeats, and great good works
buried with them: Recipes for Casserole Supreme,
Mushroom Medley, Smothered Chops, 24-Hour Salad,
Yorkshire Pudding, Prune Whip, and Chinese Chews,
are all that remain of women who spent their days
making attendance reports and flannel boards,
praying with shut-ins, passing the collection plate,
singing in Christmas pageants, reading the lectionary,
teaching communicants, planning table decorations, and
taking their signature specialties to homes of the bereaved.

In the Library

He stood at the counter, life-worn
and shabby, waiting to check out
the three thick books that looked,
to me, like more than he could carry.
He wore no coat, and worse than that,
battered moccasins without any socks.

And it was November. Now maybe
that's not saying much, considering
it was Texas, but it says enough,
if you have purple ankles and are 80—
at least I thought he was, measured
against a remembered grandpa,

who'd had the same gaunt shuffle,
bulging veins, and glassy stare.
I found out about the ankles when,
rigid as a column on the library's facade,
he began to topple sideways:
a monument collapsing.

The next-in-line supported him.
I ran to bring a chair, slipped
it beneath his meatless bones,
and watched the slow-mo
creasing of his thrift store pants
until they met the seat.

I looked down on a baby's skull
and knew I could not leave him.
The library staff called 911.
He couldn't balance in the chair.
I held him canting toward me.
It took all my strength.

He wanted to give up, lie down.
"Not here, where people can see."

In my head, my mother's voice:
"One should not do that in public!"
I knew nothing, then, of a life in which
such niceties no longer mattered.
Then someone eased him to the floor,
and spoke a quiet word that soothed
us both, and that I hadn't thought to say.
Another in the gathering crowd
turned away to pray. Something else
that, trying to help, I hadn't thought to do.

Left-Overs

One section of a Christo installation
was auctioned off last week.
Six hundred thirty dollars for a piece
eighteen feet by twenty-four.

"Running Fence" the work was called
when it sashayed silkily along
sixty-five roads, crossed forty-nine ranches,
moved with wind and rain, and, surely,
amazed cattle and horses twenty-some years ago.

The new owner says
he will fold his segment of renown
for display, in a piece of plastic wrap.
You'd think he would know better
since he flew over the installation
once in a helicopter:

an arabesque of fabric running to the sea.
Imagine such a thing being closed and creased:
a flag cased after the victory,
when the platoon has left the field;
the church lady or CEO who now
spends the day at the nursing home window;
an insect, last of its species, on a sterile metal pin.

The Nursing Home Visit

"Whoever you are, no matter how lonely,
the world offers itself to your imagination,
calls to you like the wild geese, harsh and exciting—
over and over announcing your place
in the family of things."
                    —Mary Oliver

She's propped up with pillows in a hospital bed
before which I enact a theater
of cheerful energy, meant to say, "All's well,"
though clearly nothing is. I brightly list
stops in my busy day, grumble over
workout, grocery, bank, and car repair,
then am silenced, thinking, "These small chores
are beyond her now, and ever will be."

"And what did you do next?" she kindly prompts,
as I pause, wishing I could start again,
stricken at the thought of giving pain.
Too ashamed to risk more conversation,
I grope my way in stilted monologue;
I say I've brought a favorite author's poem.
(It's Mary Oliver's "Wild Geese," one
I believe it would help to hear just now.)

But remembering the reference to going
on bared knees that comes before assurances
of each one's right to a place in life, I balk,
substitute from memory other, blander, verses.
I cannot voice those words in this time and place.
The poem I do speak leaves her unsatisfied.
The one I censor burns inside me.
We share another awkward, awful silence.

The minute hand jerks round the clock. Her eyes
close, granting me permission to withdraw;
to gather up the untapped book of poems,
my validating clutch of keys and phone;
to return to that place which I still claim, in a world
of folk who can plan, can opt, can will, can walk.

Diminished Capability

He scrawls the lines of near-iambic, born
of late night thrashings with his pillows, sheets.
At dawn, buoyed up by steaming jolts of joe,
he ignores the wanness of his conceits.

He burnishes conflated images,
with which morning pages are now rife,
and that he cannot seem to tease apart.
He hopes they are new metaphors for life.

He achieves a lofty reputation
for an increased acuity of wits,
even as his worn-out reason falters
through barren wastes, by way of empty pits.

He follows—thoughts more random, mind ever number—
the uncertain beat of an decamping drummer.

Ode to Her Computer

After reading "Ode to the Loom" by Monica Sok

Dear computer, dear HP Pavilion,
Staples's purchase,
with now outdated software,
you rest glaring on her desk
as you wait for her
to sit before you, so that,
together, you may weave
the fabrics of new poems,
both odes and elegies, as well as
sure to be ignored urgencies.

Your glow highlights her face,
frowning, as she dredges her soul
for the hurts and joys she can bear
to release. At 30 words per minute,
she sightlessly touches the letters
but still has to look if she needs
an exclamation mark. She uses lots
of those. While you obey most of her word
choices, you autocorrect when
her portmanteaux become too extreme;
and you often frustrate her searches
for pieces she is sure she has saved.

Decrepit computer, you are an old compadre
to an old woman, a god to whom
she offers oblations of time and honesty.
Yet when her wits begin to fail,
not completely, but one misspelling
at a time, and her hands no longer
bounce upon your keys
but rest, forgetful, in her lap,
will her sons carelessly dispose of you,
 unaware that you contain a hidden language,
whose Times New Roman 12 point font
made even accounts of tragedy bearable?

Or will you be taken apart
by one of her grandchildren, used
for a project bearing no relationship
to words she wrote? Will your motherboard,
who has kept her counsel, be stuffed
with regressions that will overwhelm
her shimmering words?
Will you recall how she would pause
to backspace twenty characters,
rather than highlight-and-delete, as if
what she were erasing must be scrubbed away,
too secret to be told just yet? Or will you
remember the sound of her sobs
in quiet hours when words wouldn't come?

The Changeling

The Changeling is here again today.
She is nodding, doddering, and drooled,
and though, of course, I call her "Mother,"
if she thinks she's tricked me, I'm not fooled.

That scrawny chick, with her bird-wing bones,
neither birthed me, smacked, nor hugged, nor shushed,
nor taught me how to roll my hair,
nor whom and when, I should not trust.

Gnome Baby, Age and Lost Mind's Child,
I'd find my mother if you'd just laugh,
but you giggle grimly in her chair,
your thin hair crazed, and your brown eyes daft.

If I sat beside you, tried to be kind,
would *your* mother claim you, and give me back *mine*?

Personhood Checklist

"Nobody's home but the fire, and it's out."
          —Scottish adage

Memory
Who is that singing "Melancholy Baby"
while she holds me fast in her rocking care?
Who are these bonny children running through me,
with hope in their hands, sunlight in their hair?

Time Perception
Tell me, whatever happened to Tuesday?
When did the flag of my dreams start to furl?
Wasn't there, once, a thing called tomorrow?
And wasn't I called someone's Brown-eyed Girl?

Self-Efficacy
How can I say what it is I am feeling?
Who will change me? Brush my tangled hair?
And how do I find where my home is, again?
What is the difference between here and there?

Self-Awareness
How am I me, without mirrors to see by?
Who was it spoke when I said my prayers?
What keys open these wide windows and doorways?
What is it that sits in what was my chair?

Personhood
The test has been taken? What was the score?
Unload this burden. A person no more.

The Stoic

For years you watched as your old friend
bore his burdens to the point of denial,
carried his debilities with calm certitude,
never offered complaint about his failing body.
He, although confounded by the winds
that buffeted his broken frame,
struggled on, until a pot of tea,
its lid chattering as he poured into your cup,
betrayed a cryptic palsy—tremors
he had tried to hide from you
in his little book of cares.
When a clutter of cloud befogged
his mind, as he groped for explanations, when he
could no longer tell the weeds from flowers,
still he did not recite his sorrows.
He no longer had the words.

The border wall,

recently, had thrust its obliquity
into every conversation.
How could a political argument
rend the cords that had bound them all her life?
She thought of the hateful things they'd said—
father and daughter—to one another.

She was shamed by memories of the way
she'd wrenched his words much farther to the right,
and with such asperity, he'd felt compelled
to defend positions he had never
claimed to believe. Flames of dissention
flickered at the roots of their small family.

Sheltering scarred hearts from each other's scorn,
they sat, arms folded, refusing to speak.
Blades of a fan stroked the insolent air
trying ineffectively to cool it.
His cough scolded the mucus in his lungs.

Again she reviewed their conversation,
but there was no going back: to venture
toward apology was impossible,
would require lies she could never speak.
They had allowed the world to divide them,

to eat away the principles they'd shared.
"In every wall look for the gate." Her dad
had brought her up on this aphorism.
Had his twinkle of rebellion expired
when his health and well-being were undone?

Should she forgive him his age and illness?
Make an overture? But veined hands spread out
on chair arms, mouth opened, he was sleeping.
She unpacked the basket of groceries
she had brought him and tiptoed from the house.

Environmental Concerns

My grandmother requested a lead-lined coffin
in a whispered conversation with her daughters
during her last bewildered moments. She said she feared
roots might finger the walls of a plain wood box,
work between small cracks, to reach into the chambers
of her emptied heart. She wished to "wait her Lord" intact.

"Where is she now, while she is waiting?" Mom asked,
months later, when snow had erased the name
on the newest headstone, and ice had chased the bark
of the giant elm above the family plot.
Mom and I had visited the graves that morning
at Cold Spring Cemetery, off the Lockport Road.

With evergreen wreaths we'd pieced among granite slabs
to mend our broken family. Now night closed in,
a surly sky pressed against the kitchen windows.
Mom wiped the counters and began to cry.
I pictured the markered knoll, the elm that had thrashed
above it, through so many years of winter storms.

Why had Gran, pliant before each disaster,
and in that way surviving, decided to begrudge
a tree that, surely, had been sipping our family's sorrows,
recycling its losses into the bough-bright air,
since her own mother's young bones had been folded
in the gray and stony soil, sixty years before?

When I was a child, Gran had seemed so open,
telling her life as bedtime tales: Scottish dances,
Hogmanay, and seasick passage to the new world;
yet she never spoke the painful parts: loss of mother,
death of a baby son, and early widowhood.
Though a timorous woman, she had lived resolved.

Had she always had a leaden casket
closed fast around her heart?

To the Forever Stamp in My Desk Drawer

Not content with merely waving a flag,
your designer added fireworks as well.
I cannot place you on this envelope
though you'd be less offensive than others
to be found among post office choices:
just think of Elvis with his slicked-back sneer,
seed packets with the promise of new life.
See, in addition to your festive mien,
you make the promise of eternity,
which the brief note I 'm sending will disprove
when opened by its stunned recipient.

The appropriate stamp for my sober words
would be one engraved with the plain visage
of a po-faced president: Washington,
or maybe Jefferson, whose franked image
dignified the upper right of letters
containing invites, bills, or billet-doux,
in the 1940s, as well as those
sent from houses with black wreaths on their doors.
Back then, if I am not mistaken,
there was a common purple stamp like that.
The color, too, would be appropriate,
given the cheerless news I must convey.

Rust Belt Perspectives

Late afternoon, flying in for the funeral,
looking down as we circle, waiting to land,
I see derelict heaps of slag still mar Lake Erie's shore.
From up here, the massive curves of empty granaries
are reduced to children's building blocks;
the corroded fan of the freight yard spreads
before the barren, unused terminal;
the surging path of the Niagara
still splits at Grand Island, its two arms
rejoining only to spill over the Falls;
early frost rimes the copper-green towers
of Forest Avenue; the red and yellow glory
of autumn is now a shabby blanket
beneath bared trees in Delaware Park;
graves stretch four-o'clock shadows across stiff,
brittle grasses in nearby Forest Lawn
where what's left of my raveling family
will gather tomorrow to mourn again
and to reckon who might be next to leave us.

The City of My Deaths

"Ruin is formal."
    —Emily Dickinson

Ruin is formal—
at least in Forest Lawn's stone chapel
where we mourners choke out a prayer, today,
at the brief commitment ceremony,
and then follow the hearse, through the drizzle,
to the designated plot, disturbing
a flock of gulls who've been driven inland
from the turbulent river and over
the silted canal, derelict steel mills,
decrepit downtown, to settle among
mausoleums—and stones of lesser folk.

I watch from the car as her coffin is
lowered into the baize-covered opening
to meet that of her long-beloved. Then,
one, and another, shovelsful of dirt
seal them together in their final bed,
in the city where they lived all their lives.
Everyone I love, who has died, has died
in this city.

Detached

Returning to rounds of everyday tasks,
She finds each one emptied of pleasure.
She is caught between obligations
Whose significance she cannot measure.

She's snared in a maelstrom of doubting fears,
And is besieged by inner weather.
Compared to her loss, the world's alarms
Now have the gravitas of a feather.

She turns a listless, indifferent ear
From TV's political blether,
She discerns more absence than presence
When her family gathers together.

No challenges seem to engage her;
She shuns every charge to be clever.
She cannot imagine horizons
That could tempt her today, or ever.

A woman whose very last forebear has died
Is a woman without a tether.

Spin Off

> "Thus, in our several paths, we shall still
> imitate our mother."
> > —Molière, "The Learned Ladies,"
> > > tr. by Richard Wilbur

Like a company
with dubious product lines,
our mother spun off
both her piety
and her irreverence.

I was one subsidiary.
My sister was the other.
I was the good girl,
mild, obedient, timid,
I crumbled in controversy.

Sis was made of sterner stuff.
She watched in scorn as I
yielded to a better self.
In each new conflict she held out
for her way and a licking.

We played our mother like a tune.
How could she reject the harvest
of either of our lives
when she had been the one
who'd seeded every crop?

I'm sure she did it unawares,
perhaps to still two selves at war
within the confines of her helix heart
and yet retain a stake in each.
But, in the way of things, that hasn't worked.

These days, at family reunions,
Sis and I still vie for her across the red-eyed gravy,
the congealed salads, and sweet potato pies,
trying to make memory say, at last,
who she really was.

unless
Soul clap hands and sing, and louder sing
For every tatter in its mortal dress.

How to Become a Legend in Your Own Family

Aunt Elizabeth would set the table
for my grandmother when the family gathered
to share a Sunday meal. Ever generous,
with her advice, and unaware of Grandma's scorn
for her cheese-paring ways, Aunt Elizabeth,
one Sunday, counseled, "Nell, everyone would eat less,
if you would put less on the table."

My grandmother looked at the family board
with the extra planks set in, its crisp linen cloth,
the provender she had garnered to feed
her extended family:
Elizabeth and Bob, who superintended the mill,
Bea and Harry, who did something in banking,
and of course their well-brushed children.

Nell thought about her own household:
dear Johnny, who'd lost his job to the Depression,
and worked as a Man O' Block, paid a quarter
for every sidewalk shoveled, every yard raked;
her sister and brother-in-law:
he "helped out" at his father's failing tinsmith shop,
they shared a room in Nell and Johnny's house;
and her own two girls whom she was raising
to be open-handed, for all their Scottish heritage.

"Thanks, Elizabeth, I'll remember your advice."
True to her word, every time the table extenders
were taken from the closet (Company coming!),
Nell told her daughters, and then granddaughters,
about her frugal sister-in-law.
When we had exclaimed sufficiently
about tight-wads, skin-flints, penny-pinchers,
she would unwrap an extra stick of butter
for the other end of the table.

At the dinner table

as we wait for Mom to serve the Jello,
Sis and I turn toward Gran who sits between us.
She once taught us to sprinkle lettuce leaves
with sugar, before rolling their watery
nothingness into fat stogies, even we,
confirmed vegetable-haters, might munch on.
Of the grownups we know, she is the best
at making any trial bearable.

But during this meal-time interlude,
we want to jiggle her large upper arms,
flabby pillows, both creepy, and consoling.
As a teenager she'd been a weaver
in her father's mill. Hefting yards of cloth
from table-linen looms had left her with
triceps that sagged indelicately as she aged.
These days, her muscles, turned to fat, bob
above her roughened hands, ruddy elbows:
lumps of old-lady flesh, reminiscent
of the turkeys she stuffs for Thanksgiving.

After dinner, returning to the sink,
where, hours before, she peeled potatoes
and lifted heavy kettles to prepare
the evening meal for our family of eight,
she will wash dishes, then tidy up the kitchen.

Tomorrow, in a decent print apron,
chunky shoes accommodating bunions,
she'll walk to her restaurant job where she'll use
her heavy arms to open gallon cans,
to shove dish racks through an ancient washer.
But just for now she lets us stroke them,
as she speaks to others at the table.
"Aye," she agrees with my father's comments
about a neighbor man, in words they both
deem utmost praise, "He is a hard worker."

Seventy years ago

my favorite treats
at movie theaters were
five-cent Jujy Fruits,

lemon, orange, cherry,
nasty-green, and quirky licorice;
an array of shapes:

bananas, flowers,
sheaves, berries, pea pods, fish.
A few, stamped "Heide,"

honored their maker.
Since the Heide folks never
bothered to match their forms

to the way they tasted,
I held Jujys toward the screen
blotting out Tom Mix,

Hoppy, Superman.
Flickering lights helped me choose
which ones to savor—

their colors barely
discernable against black
and white cliffhangers.

Today, at the movies,
I still eat the same candies.
(They cost a buck-fifty now,

taste of rubbery cheap perfume.)
But I still avoid the green ones,
save the black for last.

All these years I have
not changed—still want to control
what flavor's coming next.

The Hair Dresser

They gather in their cackling clusters
in my little beauty shop.
I'm the only one in the village
who will still roll up their hair.

All the other beauticians insist,
to make good money, save time,
you have got to blow dry your clients,
and move them out of the chairs.

My ladies, it's true, tend to linger,
to spend the morning right here,
once they have arrived at "La Bella,"
coming in singles and pairs.

Their canes and their walkers precede them,
I run to open the door.
Then I try to brighten their faces
with an hour or so of care.

They want to leave my establishment
with "dos" that will last all week,
but, more important, these hours are
time-off from quiet despair.

They play grandmothers' one-upmanship
with their wallets, brag books, talk:
have photos of their oldest's youngest,
or youngest's oldest to share.

Marie says this grandson's at Vassar:
men are admitted there now.
Madge says her grandchild's in Paris France,
He has a pied à-terre.

Her son "is big" in a company
that was almost bought out by. . .
now, what was that firm that went global?
Stocks were five hundred a share.

They confess that they seldom see them,
these loved ones with busy lives,
who scarcely have time for wives and kids,
much less for their parents' care.

Madge struts the room without settling.
This isn't her usual day.
She tops the pecking order Wednesdays
when here with Sally and Claire.

She's a loud and talkative woman
with a pampered, silver sheen.
My Thursday ladies, unused to her ways,
are not likely to forbear.

Madge is a good hearted old biddy,
but as with the rest of us,
when it comes to her own bad habits,
she is mostly unaware.

The sun never showed up this morning.
Now rain is slicking the street.
The steam rising from the shampoo bowl
glazes mirrors, and windows, and hair.

Gloria comes in bringing cookies.
They were intended for me,
but I offer them on the counter,
and soon, there aren't any there.

All this time I have been shampooing,
dyeing their fragile grey mops,
curling them tight in pink rollers,
to give my clients some flair.

I offer corn muffins that Millie
munches while she reports how
her sister-in-law's second cousin
has had a terrible scare,

has been diagnosed with lymphoma.
A bit of fluttering ensues,
as death enters their conversation,
a fox who's hungry and spare.

Though I try to divert my ladies
from thinking about such things,
each hen gives considered opinion:
"My, that is hard news to bear."

Madge tells of someone with something worse:
"You know that thing with the spleen.
So many months that poor man lasted!
They had to have hospice care."

Hortense roosting under the dryer
misses what Madge had to say.
She asks Arlene to repeat it all,
adds her two cents: "I declare!"

Hands keep reaching for muffins until
the box holds nothing but crumbs.
Helene picks up the "Enquirer," reads
news of a starlet's affair.

Amanda mentions a recipe
she read in "Simple Living"
that calls for a whole pound of butter.
Madge prefers simpler fare.

I begin doing Jeanette (Who is
ninety if she is a day).
She watches her hairline receding;
her confidence grows threadbare.

So I always reassure her,
"A good teasing will fix that."
Brittle hair snarls up from my comb,
As she gives the mirror a proud stare.

Then other plumes pass through my fingers,
permed-up reds, blondes, oranges, blacks
that a farmer might prize in Bantams.
I tweeze their wattles with care.

Elaine's husband's golf pro died Tuesday,
he'll be buried from St. Pete's.
With so many funerals here lately,
she knows just what she will wear.

Now some of the women are finished,
crests teased and lacquered in place.
Each works some cash from her pocket book,
preens in her helmeted hair,

finds her glasses, her walker, her boots,
and clucks about the damp cold,
puts a bill in my tip jar and asks,
"Have you a rain hat to spare?"

When Gloria leaves, the regulars
murmur, "Poor thing." "Bless her heart."
Madge says, "She didn't talk very much,
seemed to be putting on airs."

Annoyed by this interloper, friends
ruffle their feathers and peck:
"Her son's dying of. . .oh, what *is* it?"
"I know it is something rare."

"She never gets out of the house 'less
she gets a nurse to come in."
Madge, humbled, apologizing, says,
"Life is so damned unfair."

Then Gloria stands in the doorway,
tears leaking out of wide eyes.
She has come back for her umbrella,
and she blanches when hearing Madge swear.

But Madge opens arms to embrace her,
this new friend from my beauty salon.
The two find grace in their embrace,
simply by saying they care.

I got a job at a legal firm
two years after beauty school.
No one could understand why I quit,
and went back to doing hair.

Charles Burchfield: A Painter's Inspirations

"Knowledge comes, but wisdom lingers."
—Alfred, Lord Tennyson

A wood a-shimmer with the call of crows,
the dank places where hepatica grows,
clapboard houses slued on a rainy street,
a glen where winter and new life compete,

a fire thrusting against a black sky,
a bridge whose counterweight caught his eye,
sunflowers leaning in sloppy swathes,
a moon-night dance of dandelion and moths,
Orion, striding above icy trees,
charging the dark with voltaic ecstasies;

and then, when he was well into his seventies,
grumbling about his art and all its vagaries:
—why does knowledge seem to come to me so slow?—
his wife's words: "Give thanks
you've been given enough years to grow!"

Art Appreciation

"Caravaggio and His School" comes to the Kimbell Art Museum

When she first entered the world of Italian art,
she often wished she'd had the kind of childhood
(early mass, Friday fasts, nuns' sharp rulers, rosaries)
which might have put in her an eager faith
that swallowed whole, believed with head as well as heart,
the stories Baroque painters spread on canvases.
Would such a background have offered purer pleasure
than the halting, doubt-tempered, "yes-but-I" delights,
that first perturbed her before the smoky pictures
in the dim churches of Piazza 'Popolo?

Four decades later, in this crowded gallery,
amid others (out for a Sunday diversion,
or, perhaps, as intent as she on nourishment),
scruples no longer limit appreciation.
No matter if paintings she approaches feature
Francis bearing stigmata; Judith, the head
of Holofernes; Christopher, the weighty Babe;
no matter if they were made to appease faith's ardor,
or to please prelate patrons, she finds she has so schooled
herself in reading pictures that she slips at once
into the numinous, loses self in looking.

After so many years of rapt attendance,
at Depositions, Judgments, Emmaus Visits,
moments when veils were rent, dead rose, and scales fell,
she's prepared to find, in oils daubed on lengths of cloth,
a way into the sacred—even, in this room,
with its murmurings, and thoughts of early dinner.
Her incredulity, iron skepticism,
are readily subdued as awe meets effort,
at any table where she shares the Holy Meal.

Wally's Badge of Courage

Hobby night at the Old Folks' Home,
what talent did he have to show?
His collected rejection slips:
he had them laid out in a row
near others' cross stitched mats, woodwork,
postage stamps, and trapunto.

In this, His Shyness told more truth
than the rest of the world could know.
He had begun to think he created. . .
not verse, but these letters that told him, "No."

No, to hope's eager beginnings,
or to a new slant on sorrow. No,
to the scraps of others' bright joys
he had garnered to patch *his* heart whole.

"We thank you for your submission."
"Does not meet our needs at this . . . , no.
Thanks to your S.A.S.E. please
find your returned poems below."

At evening's end, he gathered his work,
returned to his room to rest.
He fingered his Participant's Ribbon,
tucked it away in his chest.
Then he began to ready for bed.
With arthritic hands he undressed.
But in the moments before his eyes closed,
he began a new poem called, "Yes."

Feathered Things

"HOPE is the thing with feathers
That perches in the soul,
And sings the tune without the words,
And never stops at all. . ."
                    —Emily Dickinson

In the wreck that is Haiti, a starving crone
treads paths made muddy by the keening rain.
She bears an empty sack, won't set it down.
She hopes one day to fill it up with grain.

In Chile, a child walks roads that used to be.
He moves through a city of dust, defeat.
He clutches shoes he prised from the debris.
His downcast eyes search for his mother's feet.

In a place where nature, as yet, is mild,
a grieving widow sees her inheritance
might be spent to aid the crone, the child,
to translate their lives into a future tense.

Our losses cast us into worlds of broken wings.
They school us in the care of others' feathered things.

Sole Mates

The rule of the dance is no one can refuse.
The bow-legged man in the scuffed cowboy boots
Asks the little old lady in tennis shoes.

Though their steps are rusty from years of disuse,
Admire his two-step, and see how she scoots!
The rule of the dance is no one can refuse.

Both know how to mind their own P's and their Q's.
Though she blushes as red as a new beetroot,
The shy little old lady in tennis shoes.

He treads on her bunions; her corns take abuse;
But her cowboy pursuer is far from a brute.
(The rule of the dance is no one can refuse.)

Now he mops his bald pate and makes his excuse,
And they sashay, and they dip, yes that old coot
And the little old lady in tennis shoes.

She's callin' him Darlin'. He whispers and woos.
No telling what steps they won't execute!
From this day on she will never refuse,
His sweet little lady in old tennis shoes.

When?

"Last can have so many meanings."
          —Dave Harris

In the window of a boutique that sold
Vuitton duffels, Hermès passport covers,
German binoculars with leather straps,
a sign inquired, "When is the last time
you have done something for the first time?"

But, as a most reluctant traveler
and an ornery resister of commerce,
fresh from reading obituaries where
my birth year figured prominently,
I transposed the words on the sign to say,

"When was the *first* time you did something
for the *last* time?" The question stopped me cold.
Perhaps it was at Uncle Walter's grave.
I was only twelve in that awful year.
But no. Think back to all those words I'd learned

by then—meeting each for the first time,
struggling to make it mine, was an adventure
that I could never have again. Just as
with each person who has enriched my life
"ave" happened only once, "vale" goes on and on.

Even though, in this life, with its crises
and crazies, I might be tempted to yearn
for the very last time I will do a first thing,
I am filled with greed to have another
last time, and then, again, one more.

The Towhee, the Scholar, and the Dog

With a cold thud she smashed against the glass,
waking *you* from drooling dreams of gourmet ducks,
and me from reveries of nightingales.
I glanced up to see oily smears upon the pane,
an eddy of dun feathers falling toward the ground.

In the yard, a stunned bird lay upon her back.
I knew you disapproved of her demeanor.
You nosed the glass and whined to tell me so.
She responded to your plaints, righting her small self,
but not before I saw her white and rusty breast.

You continued to harangue our concussed guest.
Now, unresponsive to your chiding, black eyes dull,
she made no further moves; and, wearied of scolding,
of her perverse refusal to give you an excuse
to do what you do best, you circled, flopped, slept, and

soon found dream birds more ready to consort with you
than this barely-sentient being ever could be.
I continue to stand watch. The bleak fall garden
offers no protection for the inert, ash-brown form
whose arrival roused me from Keats' frantic fantasies

(that found, in birdsong, reasons to oppose
the damming up of fluid things with names,
and to cry for laud of mystery over fact).
Her coloration says our bird's a towhee,
no stranger to our Texas neighborhoods.

Am I defying Keats by giving her a name?
I think of ode-like words I'd say if she should die.
 "She was a Towhee, tragically struck down
when she mistook the light inside my window
for *her* world's subdued, sinking autumn sun."

By making her presence known, she reminded me
that outside our cozy spheres of poetry and sleep,

another world grants entry to the pulse of life,
only if we choose to watch and listen. But, look!
The towhee's up and flying, reaching for the trees.

A bruised and unnamed bird inside me
slowly beats its wings.

The Gecko

Here is the gecko, again this morning,
trying to look like the shower curtain
to his left, the tiled wall behind him.

So quiet: this hyper-alert stillness
is what drew my eye to his pink presence.
Just a week ago we scared each other—

I by flipping on the fluorescent light,
he with his Silly Putty scuttle.
He could not know I, stomper of roaches,

slapper of mosquitoes, snuffer of spiders,
would not harm him or even trap him in
a Dixie cup and carry him outside—

this scruple something even I don't get.
How much like me does something have to be
before I squelch the instinct to remove

its nuisance and choose to consider it
a fellow traveler in this world of ours?
Did its black look, fixed on me even now,

evoke the tenderness we, as children,
learn from Disney: kindly disposition
toward the big-eyed creatures who grace our world?

Or am I wooed by his pale translucence?
Does the shadow of gut seen through his hide
suggest something of our common hungers?

A staring contest with a gecko is not
how I'd planned to start my day, but listen,
I almost think that I can hear the beat
of his three-chambered reptilian heart.

To Hope and Mrs. Oliphant

"What happiness isn't purchased with more or less of pain?"
 —Margaret Oliphant, Scottish novelist, 1828-1899

When the cataclysms happen
perturbing humankind or krill,
upending the flat land,
crumbling the thrill,
contorting the seas,
and filling them with swill,
we write to round the world again,
to smooth its folds, and still;

but the corpse of a love or a child,
brightly-burnished by our words,
laid in galley sheets,
proofed, hardbound, and blurbed,
is never interred.
Our pain is only slurred.
Earthquakes can never be exiled.
We can't write sorrow cured.

The wonder is, I thought that you should know,
my pain is eased by having told you so.

Apparent Apology

"You know better than that!"
    —Dad.

You will put your eye out
if you run with that again.
You will ruin your new shoes
playing in them in the rain.
Your face freezes like that,
There's no one but you to blame.
You will burn the house down
with that gas-fueled model plane.
Planning to wreck my car?
I have raised a scatter brain.
Aiming to flunk college?
Well, keep playing Xbox games!

Most of that stuff did not happen
to my very great relief.
I guess this is apology,
and so I will keep it brief.
As *you* prepare for parenthood
(I am awed, in disbelief),
you may regret your childhood
just because I gave you grief.
This time round, I promise I
have learned not to say a word.
I will leave you to train *your* child
with threats, I have never heard.

Focus

"focus (n.) 1640s, from Latin, focus 'hearth, fireplace'
(also, figuratively, 'home, family')."
                    —*Online Etymology Dictionary*

When he was six months old,
his mother, waking late,
found seven of us, round his blanket
on the floor, touching his fingers
and vying to be the objects
of his blessing glance. "I see,"
she laughed,
"That morning worship has begun."

At one year, Grey has pudgy breasts,
and a puppy's belly.
He barely straddles his diaper,
as he chortles across the floor.

His wobbly hip hinges let him squat, for minutes,
in positions yogi adepts recommend.
There are six tiny white pebbles
in his pumpkin grin.
His ears, from behind, stick out just a bit.
His eyes still hold us broken in their brimming blue.

Now, these are hardly the attributes of deity,
and for us he is really neither idol nor shrine,
but the hearth-place where we go to kindle hope
once more: the lens through whose eye we see
(and are seen to be)
a garden where God,
or Love, might wish to walk, again.

Skink

His quick name releases a picture
from the dictionary page
of damp earth, beside a cabin.
Gone down on what were, then,
newly-arthritic knees,
I marveled at a splay-foot treasure,
and stayed small hands
that might have crushed it
with presumptions to possess.
"Look, and let it go to make a memory."
"Oh, Grandpa!" but he did. And then,
window-gazing, on a blank November night:
"Grandpa, 'member? 'Member the skink?
I 'member!"
Such little moments. I barely brushed
the glittering scales that winked
along their backs when I tried to grab,
and—gone. But I remember.

Nomenclature

"'Please, would you tell me what
you call yourself?' [Alice] said timidly."
                    —Lewis Carroll

Both spindle-legged and Disney-eyed,
they viewed each other through the mesh.
The human baby put his hands
against the screen. "Dog," he pronounced,
mis-dubbing (as has been our species's habit,
since Adam got his naming rights)
a gift that, one way and another,
 God had brought to his very door.

I thought how men called Jesus
Elijah, Jeremiah, John,
believing that they honored Him,
though those titles fell far short
of what He would become;
and I recognized, again, my charge
to help this child name his world aright.

I stood beside him as he watched;
I whispered, "Riley, it's a fawn."
My grandchild's hand reached up for mine.
He held it tight. "Fawn," he breathed.
We named the miracle together.

Hanging the Moon from a Goal Post

When speaking of her beloved father,
and other grownups from her childhood,
my mother said, "I thought they hung the moon."
One neighbor even convinced her that he,
all alone, with a ladder and a hook,
performed that task when children were asleep.
Mom believed and lingered at the window,
on cloudless nights, to catch him in the act.

That today's children are greater skeptics
is a sad fact of my grandmother years.
Thus, you can imagine how pleased I was
when I told Riley my school colors
had been blue and orange, and he said, with awe,
"Nana, did you play football in high school?"

The Cellist's Grandfather

Listen to the music performed tonight
by the select seventh grade orchestra!
Well, at least, listen to the sounds that come
from the instruments of the performers
in the select seventh grade orchestra,
especially those sounds made by the fifth cello,
who told you, today, in the car, on the way
home from school, that his stand partner, Jeffrey,
the fourth cello, had poked him in the eye
with the end of his bow, during practice.
You try to imagine logistics
that might have made that act an accident,
then try not to remember that his parents have spent
nine hundred bucks on this three-fourths cello
he has outgrown ten weeks into the year;
that he has missed his private make-up class
for three weeks running because of swim meets.
Concentrate on how he looks at home,
afternoon sun streaming behind his head,
his fingers arched on frets, his bow arm curved—
when he does remember to practice;
how he plays his favorite pieces again
and again, his face unwrinkling with each note.
Tell his parents, "He has come a long way!"

Somewhere in Texas,

in the small house, one rainy afternoon,
my grandson asked, "Which are you better at:
planning ahead or fixing what goes wrong?"
I pulled my hands from the sudsy dish pan,
dried them, and reflected on his question.
The kitchen smelled of grilled cheese sandwiches,
somewhat scorched, which we had shared for lunch,
after hours of reading Harry Potter.

"Planning," I said, as I balanced, with regret,
the anguished days that prefaced every choice,
against my panic when missteps required
that I make spontaneous revision.
"What about you?" (I knew this eight-year-old
liked questions for which he had the answers.)
"I'm pretty good at both. I like to plan,
but if I mess things up, I can fix them,"
was his immodest, but truthful, reply.

The *Order of the Phoenix* lay book-marked
on the sofa, waiting our return.
Was the Boy-Wizard's mishap with his wand
the source of Ryan's question, or was it
the sandwiches with their over-charred bread?
In that house newscasts were never permitted.
The world's catalog of horrors did not
present itself. Truths were learned in storybooks.

As late as August, Two Thousand and Five,
when "Mistakes Were Made," at every level,
and no one raised a hand to say, "My fault,"
as our institutions huffed and sputtered,
looking for direction, but finding none,
 this boy knew that he had ability
to acknowledge error and learn from it,
and that, in the world beyond his small house.
he could misstep, make amends, and still achieve.

At the Waco Wendy's, After the Poetry Festival

Because our vocabularies are sufficient to describe
your skimpy dresses as harlequin, lamé, or Prussian blue;
because we have studied ancient myth and can read you as
three graces, not simply as one lithe and two rounder girls;
because we have seen enough in our long lives to rejoice
that the tallest among you wears dyed-to-match stilettos;
and trained in irony, can contrast kids behind the counter,
flipping burgers, with you, and your brand-new shimmer;

when your dates begin to clown, lift their hands and wave
so you will watch them tap-dancing at the drink-lid station,
we curtail our talk of metaphor as the looking glass of life,
set down our sandwiches, enjoy your easy antics,
and file poets' briefs on the sweetness of this evening:
the late sun piercing plate glass, to glaze your heedless joy.

Thanks to our craft we're able to attend to your experience,
to parcel into a few lines what, for one of you, might become
the moment you'll remember as the beginning of everything,
and to concoct from our words a poultice strong enough
to warm life's thinning threads.

Bacchus in Texas

Bacchus, a terracotta mask,
grimaces, gape-mouthed
on the garden wall.
He's an expatriate under our live oaks,
although the sun sets as outrageously here
as it did behind the black cypresses
and the raw ocher oven
where he was once fired.

Moss has worked its way into his frown,
has given a cast to one of his eyes
and split the curl of his lip.
Grandchildren watch him warily,
especially when one girl is brave enough
to tease the daddy-long-legs
quartered in his throat.
Then, their pulsing communion disturbed,
the critters whisker down his chin.

Bacchus and I rarely converse now
about the old days,
but, at the Feast of the Assumption,
Ferragosto, we usually remember
how the heat of a Roman summer
would explode the cones of the umbrella pines,
graveling a dusty piazza with pignoli.
And, last year, when a spider webbed
a monocle over his bad eye,
I took his picture.

Comportment

I saw her first when glancing down the hill,
a doe cavorting with the neighbor's dog.
But when the mastiff fled, I read the scene again.
A mad deer then, who'd dared engage that rogue.

Next morning, she challenged me. In the yard,
She blocked the path that led out to the street.
Planting her bulky flank, athwart my way,
she stared me down and stamped her brittle feet.

I thought to call the City to report,
"Deer behaving strangely on Bowie Lane."
Her eyes burned with a care I could not read;
her mouth was grim. She matched her will with mine.

I saw her through the screen again, today,
the alert Y of ears and eyes and snout:
a clement doe who d brought her fawn to see
an old and foolish woman who'd forgot

maternal fierceness trumps the expectation
of behavior that is seemly and sedate.
Why should it matter if the mother is
a homo sapiens or an ungulate?

Growing Season

For no special reason he chose
the blue bowl to collect the okra.
It had long sat, dusty, neglected,
in the highest of the kitchen cabinets—
too far for his wife to reach,
and too wide for her small hands.

But each fall, tending his garden,
when he had watched the blowsy flowers
morph into pentagonal jewels,
he would lift down the blue bowl, again,
a freebie from a box of soap,
that fit just right in his broad palms,

would walk the emerald rows, reaching,
plucking, setting each green gift
in the Bakelite vessel
that he carried back to the house:
a provender to be enjoyed
at dinner, after thanks were given.

The Ritual of Friendship

Old ladies,
who sit together in church,
(veined hands gripping hymnals,
canes tucked almost under pews,
but still visible so they will not
be forgotten after worship),
know each other's afflictions,
remember each other's husbands,
the whereabouts of each other's grandchildren,
the Sunday School misbehaviors
of each other's children, decades ago,
and thus, find comfort in each other's
presence
as the Communion plate is passed,
and as they whisper with their whole hearts,
"The body of Christ broken for *you*,"
each reassured that God remembers her
because her name is on the tip
of the other's tongue.

Why We Don't Give Each Other Gift Certificates

Walking rooms I've spruced up for my sister-guest,
I give pride of place to gifts she's given me.
On kitchen shelves, Deruta pots are gleaming.
Pantry oils and spices, speak of her largesse.
My office is scented with a wreath of bay.
I've placed the handmade mirror in the front hall,
the bright amaryllis in the dining el,
Little Women in the room where she will stay.

I am always grateful when I visit her:
She still wears the pin, displays the antique doll,
And muddles her drink with the silvery stir.
We are each other's oldest friend. Who else could
(With our forebears and our girl pals lost to time)
cherish both each other's now and our childhoods?

Breastworks

1. The Tell

Having cancer is a bit like being pregnant,
the way it was once: the first weeks a great secret
granting time to integrate a crucial notion
into one's understanding of who she might be.

I did not want to know what everyone thought, or
claimed to think, before I reached my own conclusions.
I was not ready to evert my private life.
I hoped to write the hash tags for my own pain.

By keeping mum, I favored solitude over
solicitude, neither one a pleasant option.
Yet to keep the cancer a secret might give it
more power than would speaking of it.

I was not shamed by the disease, a fault, perhaps
in genes. But I do try to lead a fuss-free life.
I felt that I would let myself, and others, down
if I should be perceived as needing care.

"Have you told anyone about your cancer?"
my sister asked. And then, "Why ever not?
Do you think that your not speaking of it
will magically cause it to disappear?"

But then I took a doctor's call while at the gym,
in a quiet corner where no one else would hear,
except the small, odd man who sat there every day.
"You the person having surgery?" he hollered,

as I completed my furtive call. Though compelled
by good manners, I bristled even as I answered—
my secret was out, and not of my own choosing.
"Well, then, I'll pray for you," he promised.

I can no longer deny myself the comforts
that will come with the sympathy of others,
despite the wagging tongues for which I'll be a topic:
a cancer declaration will, no doubt, invite

friends to tell me of my bright appearance, before
they huddle to confer (I've often done the same)
about how life is catching up with me.
"God love her, she's. . .not looking very good."

But to let friends rattle on about their hangnails
and their hurt feelings, as I measure their woes
against my own unspoken trials, is, I see, unkind.
Releasing my secret, I open my heart to love.

2.   Pink

Did you see me today at the market
waving ahead the woman with five items?
At the stop sign, politely taking my turn?
In the clinic, with a patient smile
for the clerk who mis-booked my appointment?
I'm obviously much too nice a woman
to have a tumor in her breast.

But this afternoon a neighbor at my door
presented me a blanket made by his wife, who
crippled by her cancer, spends her last days
at home doing good for other folks like me.
The blanket is pink, a color I loathe,
and comes with an implication I reject:
that she and I are sisters in our plight.

Now let's see how kind a person I am.
Will I wrap the blanket round my shoulders
between treatments, on reflective afternoons,
and value a good woman's care of me?
Or will I pen my thank you letter
and bury this offence in a back closet
still not ready to be as mortal as my neighbor?

3. Kintsugi

Kintsugi is the art of repairing broken pottery
with a joining of gold.

When the lady, startled, let drop
the precious vase ("It just fell from my hand,"
 she cried, dabbing at her eyes
with the sleeve of her kimono),
the craftsman used a golden joinery
to patch the broken places.
The brew of lacquer, flecked by gilt,
was not administered with stealth.
The break was not to be forgotten,
but honored with a forthright application
which said, "Just here in its existence, this object
sustained calamity that must be
memorialized by precious metal,
an unguent piecing broken bits,
saturating cracks, even replacing
fragments lost forever to the tatami floor."

As part of an ongoing story,
the mended crevice glitters, the gold tooth
in an otherwise perfect smile.

Just so, the brokenness I have endured,
the failing body, rehabbed hopes,
cannot be sealed with some invisible
Gorilla Glue, nor carted to the attic
to be attended at a later time.
The flux of golden words,
the shining acts of kindness,
the laying on of hands,
that have honored both my pain
and its release, must somehow be allowed
to gleam through me:
an aureate seam declaring what has happened,
that my experience might also be
part of a story that continues.

4. Kintsugi, Too?

"There is a crack in everything."
        —Leonard Cohen

There is a crack in everything?
I wish that there were only one,
But, by 80, all is slivers,
We know our time is nearly done.

Buddhist thinking has an answer.
How should one deal with aging's cracks?
By revising and repairing.
If you are wounded, struggle back.

In Eastern thought, each broken plate
Should be spectacularly glued.
A bright and blatant seam of gold
Should be applied where flaws intrude.

This patching is a sacred rite,
It doesn't try to hide the craze,
Accepts the process now begun;
And consecrates by giving praise.

While in the West most people choose
To cover up each fractured dream
With brighter bow ties, makeup smears,
A tub of Rocky Road ice cream.

Internal Memo

You say, "The world's precisely what it seems,
a game of chance that's rigged against the weak."
Who says that I must live such downsized dreams

of loss's sobs and violation's screams,
of hungers like a raptor's ready beak?
You say, "The world's precisely what it seems,"

but I say, "Love's an anguish that redeems,
that douses thirsts, and magnifies the meek."
Who says that I must yield to downsized dreams,

declaring man unworthy of esteem
while caught in God's sly game of hide and seek?
When you say, "Life's precisely what it seems,"

I say, "From secret chasms, mercy streams."
I evoke the beauty of a child's cheek.
Who says that I must sleep with downsized dreams?

Despite your desperate dark, my hope still gleams.
Though you point out the ugly, brittle, bleak,
though you say life's precisely what it seems,
who says I must accept *your* downsized dreams?

Household Economy

One half of our Christmas cactus
is pouring out its heart on a kitchen shelf
in vermilion, triple-layered blooms.
The other half, though glossy-green,
has nothing to say for itself this December.
Cladodes of both halves drape, succulent,
over the edge of their pot,
facing away from each other.
The responsibility for the inconsistency is mine.
Last spring, tired of other years' scraggly stems,
I combined two dusty plants on the patio
before I exposed them to the bright Texas sun.

It seems their pot-bound wedlock hasn't worked.
I'll refrain from seeing symbolism here
of a misalliance where two householders
are so very out of sync.
And yet—perhaps this planting does reflect
the secret of another kind of union:
the marriage where he holds on
as his wife goes to pieces;
or her joy infects his numbness
till he can get a grip.

The pot is not a pretty picture
with its lopsided presentation.
Later in the winter it will, no doubt,
mirror today's disharmonies,
when the now-sullen stems
decide to bloom in startling shades of shrimp,
and all that remains of the present bliss
will be some brown and brittle tufts.
At that moment, I will think, again,
about biorhythms, psychic seasons,
and sending in the clowns.

Leaving Our Mark

"That will be us in twenty years," she hissed,
to her spouse, seeing Jack and me on the patio,
bundled in sweaters, on that mild fall day,
too frail leave while they looked at our place.

Perhaps we suggested their recklessness:
Buying a big house for the two of them,
with family raised, and careers at an end,
was like spitting straight in the face of time.

"A one owner house," the listing proclaimed,
meaning we old folks who were watching them,
with our confused mixture of hope and dread,
had been the first to laugh or shed tears here.

They ignored the question our presence posed:
Why buy this place when, in just a few years,
old age will force you to move once again?
They signed papers, claimed what had been our home.

Soon, wallpaper, popcorn ceilings, were gone,
and silk drapes were swapped for new metal blinds.
Shelves scuffed by a thousand books were painted
to hold golfing trophies and souvenirs.

Baseboards, nicked by our walker and wheel chair,
and dog-stained carpets were placed at the curb,
cracked windows reglazed, chimney sweep called in.
A door mat gave greetings in twenty tongues.

Their audacious kitchen renovation
with budget-breaking granite countertops,
included a side-by-side fridge with room
for photos of their own family and pets.

They thought they had wiped our memory away
with all it said of the passage of time,
but when spring came, they turned to the garden
and found we were still part of the place:

Easter lilies, prized gifts from our children,
emerged, fragrantly, in row after row;
redbud trees planted, one for each grandchild,
began to open, impossibly pink.

The blue bonnet patch spoke of memories
of family photographs for fifty springs,
it was our blooms that lured bright butterflies,
our Esperanza that reached for the eves.

Each sprouting plant a reminder of us:
seeds we had harvested, cuttings from friends.
They found dog bones buried in every bed,
and one afternoon, the bones of a dog.

Fine Things

Fine Things are reservoirs for the heart.
                    —Fennel Hudson

Last night, on an edgy TV drama,
a wealthy man who was about to die
walked through his sumptuous home for one last look.

At the mantle he touched an objet d'art:
a blue and gold enameled horse, much loved,
to judge by the regret that creased his eyes.

The actor had the moment's mood just right:
the man said good-bye, not to his treasure,
but to a life where such things signified.

As he laid the back of his hand, gently,
on the horse's thigh, frozen in mid-prance,
I felt as if my own hand grazed the beast.

I imagined the last walk I will take,
one day, through the world of my belongings,
things no one else could love as well as I.

Will I stroke the cool flanks of hand-thrown pots
whose luscious glazes, secret-keeping shapes,
I've sought around the world for 60 years?

Will I let my eyes fall on paintings, prints,
whose selection always required that
some other loveliness be left behind?

Will I caress carvings whose every crevice
I have dusted, oiled, and come to love
for memories imbedded in their wood?

Will I unfold fabrics woven with care;
by the artisans of Nigeria,
Italy, Ghana, Scotland, and Japan,

and quilts that were stitched by my mother,
in decades gone; to offer gratitude
for color and craft that inhere in them?

Will even the silver, unpolished for years,
whose pattern-selection took weeks of thought,
receive my thanks for its having mattered?

Something to Hang Onto

Your mother's finger as you learned to walk;
The silky ear of your snuggle bunny
When you were sent to your room for your sass;
The book of poems your father gave you
The Christmas before he passed away;

The handlebars of your second-hand bike
When you reared back to pop your first wheelie;
The street car strap when you could finally reach it;
The edge of your battered seventh-grade desk
As you stood to recite "Flanders' Fields;"

The baby-sitting dimes stuffed in your purse,
On your first solo trip downtown;
The rolled-up diploma stamped with your name;
The heart-signed memo, left on the counter,
You discovered while grabbing your keys;

The small fingers that reached up to grasp yours
As their owner took his tipsy first steps;
A photo album with black and white snaps;
The scruffy pup who paced beside you
When a child was late coming home from a dance;

Your beloved's hand before the casket closed;
A friend's shoulders, when her life had soured;
Your integrity as rumors ran wild;
The dark arm that offered to link with yours
While protesters sang, "With One Voice;"

The seamed palm of the stranger beside you
As the whole congregation passed the Peace;
The wafer a nun brings you, a Protestant,
On your first sad week in the nursing home;
When you remember to look for it, always,
Something to hang onto.

Georgia O'Keeffe, a Life in Perspective

Flowers were one focus of her early years:
poppy, iris, canna, morning glory.
She pollinated their potential
with the furry legging of her brush;

and she saw the mountains with an eagle's eye,
her brush becoming a cataclysm
that heaved rock and fissure on to canvas
beneath a line of broad and shining sky.

When even those perfections did not provoke the gods,
she mastered clouds, looking down upon them
from far above the flowers and the mountains.
Her brush, a serene whip, ordered their serried rows.

But the vision that had been, by turns,
apian, aquiline, divine,
began to fail. She set her brush aside,
allowed assistants' hands to do her work.

Across a room, severe, and stripped of objects,
through whose windows she could no longer see
the jimson weed, the valley road, the stars,
her eyes groped for the golden, graceful hand

mounted on the fireplace's white-washed flank:
a long-fingered Buddha's palm curved in a gesture
that spoke the dharma she had lived by all her life:
"Fear not!"

L'Heure Bleue

L'heure bleue is the hour between day and night
when flowers are said to smell sweetest.

Now comes the blue hour.
And look, across the plain,
The future is coming toward us.
Or is it only rain?

Now comes the blue hour.
The day will cede her reign.
The moon will cross the blackened sky.
She too is on the wane.

Now comes the blue hour.
Have done with strife and gain.
Your hopes like crops are all laid by,
And your regrets in vain.

Now comes the blue hour.
It's big with wistful pain.
Take care against temptation of
The needle in the vein.

Now comes the blue hour.
Don't watch it through the pane.
Step out onto the garden walk.
Here are your shawl and cane.

Now comes the blue hour.
There's no need to feign.
It's not easy to cross the verge,
And yet we must, we twain.

Now comes the blue hour.
Rosemary, mint, vervain:
How beautiful crushed flowers smell,
As they pass in the horse-drawn wain.

His Dog

She's at the door every day, when I get home from work.
Well, of course, she is.
Haven't I fed her earlier and earlier each evening,
Since we've been alone?
He would say that I'm spoiling her.
But deprived, myself, I want to give her what I can.
So she's there, just to remind me to put kibble in her bowl.
Though she does sit politely beside me, until I say, "Okay!"

She is beside my chair whenever I sit down.
Well, of course, she is.
Always wants to be near the fire. My chair is the closest.
Though she does sit beside his chair when, occasionally,
I creep into it to ease my loneliness.
But then, she always was his dog.

She whines at night when I close the bedroom door.
Well, of course, she does.
She's always had an eye out for a more comfortable bed.
Why settle for cold tile if she might get access to the carpet
In our—my—room? I wish my needs were as simple as hers.

She is still outside that door in the morning.
Well, of course, she is,
Offering a persistent paw to greet me until I stoop to pet her.
She's attention hungry. How he was played by her appeals.

She tries to crawl into my lap when I drive her to the kennel.
Well, of course, she does.
He let her get away with anything.
What a nuisance. She should realize we've both lost him now.

After one long day, I pick her up.
Well, of course, I do.
She tugs her leash from the handler's grip, runs to greet me,
As the vet observes, "Oh, how she has missed you."
Well, of course, she has.

Fur Coats

For some 30 years they'd shared a clothespress
under the rafters: Grandmother's beaver,
Great Aunt's Persian lamb, once worn by women
who traveled our town, by street car and bus,
neither one having learned to drive a car.
This closet, a museum, of sorts, housed
Eastern Star evening gowns, spent eider downs,
moth-eaten linens from grandfather's mills,
my own wedding dress: objects too dear
to place at the curb, or send to Good Will.

When our mother died, my sister and I,
readying the house for an estate sale,
opened the clothespress whose moth ball odors
scarcely hid a whiff of some creature's lair.
As each of us slipped on an antique fur,
we were the ladies from decades ago.
How had the two wizened souls we recalled
ever withstood the great weight of these coats,
while traversing the perilous sidewalks
of our blustering Buffalo winters?

Sis and I regarded each other. Dressed
in garments of forebears, we seemed
to inhabit their lives: the older one
widowed early, had the more cautious purse.
The other, recklessly conscious of style,
preened on her way to department store jobs.
Those days there was no PETA to report
the horrors involved in factory farms,
to say the lambs' soft curly wool had been
skinned from babies ripped from their mothers.

In terms of their dress, our ancients had been
much closer to hunting-gathering folk
than they were to the great-great grandchild, who,
a vegan since birth, now wears canvas shoes

even when going to job interviews.
And then we remembered other trophies
borne by the shoulders of our women folk:
the leopard-skin coat our mom had sported
all through the 'Forties, then turned inside out:
"Fur as a lining is a more Fifties look."

And the silver fox stole our dad bought her:
two four-foot long bodies, complete with tails
and glass eyes—eventually deemed "too much."
How my sister and I had soothed ourselves
by stroking those pelts on endless car trips!
Being the older, I also recalled
an earlier stole made from several skins—
with dangling legs, tipped by tiny toe nails—
so cleverly held together by clips
sewn where their mean little jaws should have been.

We replaced the coats, with their monogrammed
linings, on soft, padded hangers, unsure,
what we should do with these tribal relics,
as we prepared to close the family home.
Then a newspaper ad netted a call
from a woman who fashioned gloves and boots
with furs scavenged from just such outré pelts.
She would take our memories, pick them apart,
and stitch them into other folk's clothes.
But our stories seem stuck in that closet,
in a house with new paint and new owners,
on a street we'll never visit again.

A Ghost's Story: At the Estate Sale

"Her fingertip veil fell from a bonnet of illusion
to match her gown."
           Buffalo Evening News, February 21, 1943

The modest bridal veil is laid out on the bed,
(Estate sale agents often stage the clothes this way),
As if it's ready to be slipped on some bright head.

"The owner's in a nursing home, or so it's said.
What if her spirit should recall her wedding day,
And return to don the veil laid out on the spread?"

"Oh, look, the veil is trimmed with beads and silken thread.
How quaint. Today its ruffles look a little gray,
Seems a bit shabby to be slipped on a bright head."

"This old clipping marked sixty years since she was wed.
She's pictured with her husband—eighty, if a day.
Just think what stories could be told by this old bed!"

"Here's a journal that describes the girl, the life she led.
It's a record of her bride dreams on that lost day,
Hours before she slipped the veil on her bright head.

"She writes her veil's 'as dainty as a whipped parfait,'
As she awaits the soldier boy with her bouquet . . ."

As someone buys the veil laid out on my old bed,
Hands gently close my vacant eyes, cover my white head.

Amos Profet

"That which we are, we are."
  —Alfred, Lord Tennyson

They buried my ashes here, by the overlook parking lot,
the very place I came each Monday with a garbage sack
and a nail stick to walk the trail. Folks used to say, "Amos,
wouldn't it make more sense to walk the trail first,
and clean it up on the way back?" But after I'd seen the view,
I never wanted to look at garbage. I didn't mind toting it,
I just didn't want to look at it.

So I bagged the trash on the way in, hauled it back out.
I was good at hooking Bud cans, coffee cups,
but them candy wrappers never stayed on the nail.
Somehow, I couldn't get purchase to pick them up. What
were they made of? It wasn't paper; it wasn't plastic either.
I knew *people* like that. Neither one thing nor another.
You spoke to them directly, they didn't engage.
They slithered away like a candy wrapper from a nail stick.

Speaking of slithering, I always wore a pair of gloves out here.
I'd seen snakes, big around as my wrist, snoozing in the sun.
I feared someday I'd reach down for a wrapper and come up
with one of them. And danged if that wasn't what happened.

Well, I can see that you're thinking, "He's quite the talker."
Mary, my first wife, used to say, "Amos, just let folks be!
Give them a minute to think their own thoughts, without
wearing them out with yours!" But you know what I think?
If you have something to say, say it. Big mouth, blow-hard,
windbag, I've been called all of that, but if you know something
somebody else don't, why shouldn't you tell them,
as I did when I worked on the Santa Fe.
—And if people are fools, why pretend that they aren't?

The problem with the folks who come out here is this:
they use this place as a get-away, not a go-to, but a get-away.
My coffin didn't lie in a church. I haven't been in one

in 40 years. Not since my youngest. . . . But I still know
everybody needs a place for going-to. This, here, was mine,
 even before I died. If you are using a place as a get-away,
well, you don't care what kind of trash you leave behind.

Why some folks, kids mostly, actually read their I-Phones here.
Now I ask you, who would walk out into this bright world
while staring at one of them? But they do. I have even found
some of them phones left behind, their screens smashed to stars.
What kind of kid, do you suppose, doesn't have parents
who would give him hell if he lost something like that?
I can only hope those phones were misplaced
when someone lifted his face up from one of them,
and was so taken by what he saw around him
that he forgot what he had been looking at.

Well, you'll see, just around the bend there, and up the rise.

A Woman's Life

A woman's life is memorialized
by the fabrics that have passed through her hands:
the Hudson Bay blanket pulled up and tucked;
damp sheets hissing under her iron;
soft towels she has fluffed and folded in thirds;
placed in fragrant piles near shower and tub;
by rags that hang limp on the lip of a sink,
after a good scrub and polish,
and muslin that soaks up splashes and stains
when the canning is done for the year.

A woman's life is memorialized
by point d'Alençon, a blue garter;
by argyle socks, darned on ivory eggs,
pearl buttons affixed to fine, cambric shirts,
by her choice of chintz curtains, silk swags,
and a mauve velvet divan for the parlor;
in her sure passage through Winn's fabric shop
as she seeks for percale, and dimity,
then pauses to fondle a bolt of blue flannel,
thinks, "Is it too soon to buy some of this?"

A woman's life is memorialized
by receiving blankets scented with milk,
diapers, buntings, and footed pajamas,
little girls' dresses twitched straight in doorways,
the backs of boys' collars tugged down;
pleated skirts lengthened, khakis patched at the knee;
by ten pairs of gauzy butterfly wings
sewn in one night for the second grade play;
by tee-shirts, tutus, prom dresses, tuxes,
on which, for a few years, she's asked to consult.

A woman's life is memorialized
by the wrinkled attempt Mary once made
to construct her first Home Ec. skirt,
a garment that earned a county fair ribbon
when tweaked by her mother's deft fingers;

by patchwork pieced in moments of grace
when the day's many chores were accomplished,
and navy serge was paired with pink poplin,
then secured with the small, patient stitches
that spoke of her loving precision.

A woman's life is memorialized
by crisp linen hankies in a pocketbook,
fine denier nylons in a lingerie drawer,
a worn gingham apron hung by the stove;
the plaid, belted bathrobe she wore near the end;
and, at last, by the blue crêpe de chine,
discovered at the very back of her closet
with the price tag still pinned to the sleeve.
They crossed her hands on its brocade bodice,
a dress saved for a special occasion.

Karma

1.
Dug from the river bed, the soft white clay
was freed of pebbles, gravel, and sand.
The craftsman beat it again and again,
until it flowed beneath his hand.

The argil he'd wedged, he slapped on the wheel
and fostered into a small fluted bowl
that endured the happenstance of the kiln
to emerge unwarped, gracious, whole.

The simple vessel, glazed and refired,
was displayed in a shop by the potter.
I purchased it, a souvenir of my trip,
a gift to mother from daughter.

2.
After the peach tree was nourished with meal,
though expected winter rains never fell,
its pink buds, still furled, escaped the last frost,
then with the spring began to swell.

Worker bees buzzed by at the proper time.
The greenish drupes throve in the dazzling sun.
Earwigs and borers gave the fruit a pass—
its knobs, by then, a rosy dun.

Though when plucked, some bumped a basket's edge,
they still charmed me at a roadside display.
I placed them, for Mom, in my grocery sack,
the day before she passed away.

3.
Now, after the memorial service,
I stand alone in her lifeless kitchen,
and from the smooth-spun, honey-hued bowl,
as I lament, as my heart is riven,
I select a blond peach with its brown bruise:
the one comfort this moment has given.

Revenants

An old woman in a pink pantsuit,
waving a long, Kelly green scarf,
has been showing up in my dreams ever since
the first night after Mother died.
She smiles, then scurries through my sleep, trying
to catch a bus to somewhere else.

The spring after Uncle Ray died, my aunt claims,
a rabbit came to her back garden.
She offered it carrots that it never ate.
Six years later it still returns.
She finds it sitting in the grass, alert
under the flowering crab tree.

She tells it how hard the winter has been,
names small victories, great losses,
reads to it from her devotional book.
I thought her daft when she first told me this,
but then, I found droppings under the tree.

The pantsuit of the sprite that visits me
is pink as the blooms on my aunt's apple tree.
I 'm almost used to her patrolling my dreams,
in the old neighborhoods of my mind;
I wish she'd stop to chat, at dawn or at three.
Those seem to be the darkest of times.

But she's forever flagging down buses
with that scarf of hers. I'd like to take it
from her, wrap it round me—a green prayer shawl—
and ask her in for tea—now that
I've figured out she's come to comfort me
in my first motherless winter.

Quilting Suite

Every year I make my pilgrimage
to a cathedral of the homely arts.
For days, our noisy Expo Center
is transformed by muted celebration.
In sets of three, sheets of black muslin
are hung to make secluded chapels.
And women ambulate among them,
entering each station to regard
bright windows mounted, one per panel,
that shimmer jewel-like on ersatz walls.
How hushed the conversations of these women
who are both makers and acolytes.
Skilled critique of one another's work
brims with tribute for their common art.

My mother, loved to dazzle friends by piecing
unlike fabrics with careful stitches,
to feel the crisp hand of a new-sewn quilt.
I know she'd like to be with me, today,
standing before these coverlets,
akin to other expert women,
sharing the arcana of nine-patch,
broderie, log cabin, stack-and-whack.
Loss of sight ended her membership
in this sisterhood. Her quilts never
found a place in this cathedral, but
descendants dream beneath them every night.

Blending solitude and company,
a sacred society of quilters
is much like any band who tend
 a holy fire: lonely hours spent
cutting, stitching a thousand pieces,
balanced by assemblies of friends
who, gathered at the quilt, sew backing,
batting, and top to one another.
Cards pinned to every counterpane describe
the sweet interplay of work and prayer:

"Three friends made this quilt in different colors."
"I worked this one while I was taking chemo."
"This prairie rose was my first best in show,"
proclaim sacred texts of this communion.

A bed turning is about to start:
Women stand either side of a heap
of quilts. One tells the story of each work.
Helped by her friend, she flings a cover back.
As if relics were to be unveiled,
she displays a wonder that has cost
two hundred hours of her life. Time
she might have spent with spouse, grandchildren,
but that she gave instead to her exacting craft.
She says her beds and walls are layered
at least five deep with such masterpieces,
her cats have favorite ones to sleep on.
White angora hairs prove what she says.
I marvel at her dedication.

Yet, should I find such devotion strange?
Composing a poem, do I not leave
letters unsent, beds unmade, to seek
the-very-words in my bag of scraps?
I think again of my mother's quilts,
that never collected a prize in a show,
and yet, were the work she had to do,
essential to her getting on with life.
From hers and these examples, I can learn
obedience to beauty and to craft.

Ownership

After breakfast, one spring morning
in the little house on Elm,
your dad whipped you twice for sassing him,
thumbed tears and egg smears from your face,
smoothed and kissed your cow lick,
and sent you straight to school.

Fifty-two years later, your dad is gone.
His funeral was yesterday.
The Elm Street House now only that,
another piece of real estate.
Soon the finger prints of strangers' children
will claim the doorways and the walls.
You lock up one last time, tack a Sold sign
to the railing on the porch, and walk up town.

Cardinals mark the blue air with song.
The town's oldest dog, a gnarled feist,
pees importantly on a post
that's already damp and reeking,
near your agency at Maple and Main.
In the office you draw up deeds for two choice lots
in your new development: Lake Howard.
You named it for your dad.

Each of us finds his own ways
of declaring, "This is mine!"

Ode on a Backyard Tree

I once read the "Ode on a Grecian Urn,"
standing on a path beside a live oak tree.
Then, stepping closer through the spongy earth,
I read again—my hand touching her brittle bark.
I chose this poem for its remembered reference
to eternal boughs whose leaves could not be shed.
I thought to celebrate her permanence,
for I had watched her, steadfast through mad gales,
much like the ones that hurled my life about,
and I had been emboldened to persist
by knowing that her roots did not let go.

Yet as I read the first time, I glanced up
and noticed how her rugged limbs were thrashing,
on that bright but blustery day,
how her branches declined to leafy fringe,
whose turn to sepia from green had just begun.
And when I read the second time, I felt
the brede of mossy plants across her bark.

She was not immune to time as were those boughs
carved in marble that Keats immortalized.
Though near-eternal from my curtailed view,
each year she released wearied leaves,
dropped new catkins to stain the graveled walks,
offered nesting for a different clutch of squirrels,
rained a fresh crop of acorns on my roof.

Even the sunlight that fell upon the text
of the poem I read for her was filtered
by the dynamics of her shifting leaves,
modulated by the November breeze.
And setting poets' whims aside, I saw
that she was snared in time as much as I,
and that her staunch demeanor offered me
consolation, only because I knew,
one day, she, too, would be uprooted, overthrown.

The breeze toyed with her branches, yet again.
Her wind chime throbbed, a solitary note.

Or set upon a golden bough to sing
To lords and ladies of Byzantium
    Of what is past, or passing, or to come."
        —William Butler Yeats "Sailing to Byzantium"

Discussion Questions

1. If Old Age were a foreign country, would these poems serve as a travel brochure or a State Department Travel Advisory?
2. What are some of the difficulties of the aging experience reflected in this collection?
3. What are some of the joys and consolations of aging highlighted in these poems?
4. Most of the people who speak in these poems seem to confront only personal problems. What insights does this collection offer to a world beset by pandemic and civil strife?
5. Which of these poems most accurately reflect your ideas of aging?
6. Which poems do you think voice the author's own perspective on aging?
7. Some of these poems regard aging from a humorous perspective. Is that appropriate given the serious nature of most of the collection?
8. Given that most of the poems are voiced by people caught up in the experience of aging, what is the reason for poems told from the perspective of a mask, a chambered nautilus, a burnt-out church?
9. Contrast the aspects of aging that seem most important to the elderly characters in the poems with those that seem more salient for their families and caregivers.
10. Is there a character in one of the poems with whom you would like to have a conversation about aging? Who? Why?

The author is grateful to the friends who helped design these discussion questions: Carol, Jill, Donna, Pat, Pearl, Susan, Vicki, and Jean.

www.ingramcontent.com/pod-product-compliance
Lightning Source LLC
Chambersburg PA
CBHW021506090426
42739CB00007B/489